THE
Monday
Morning
CLUB

You're Not Alone
Encouragement for Women in Ministry

CLAUDIA BARBA

Published by Press On! Ministries, 9345 Brookville Road, Indianapolis, IN 46239.

www.ipresson.com

Printed in the United States of America.

ISBN 978-0-9914576-1-8

To David, my beloved.
Wherever you are, that's where I want to be.

Table of Contents

Chapters by Topic

What to read …

Introduction

The days of a woman in ministry overflow with the best and the most challenging experiences life can offer. If you're a wife in ministry, you have a visible but mostly undefined job--one of the least understood roles a woman can play.

I have watched you at work. I see you serving Christ with grace and joy; I marvel at your selflessness in serving His people. But I know it's not always easy, and that even a little bit of help from someone who understands can go a long way.

Your Heavenly Friend does understand. He once lived where we live, so He knows what it's like to work with human beings. The promises in His Word encourage us. He also brings us comfort through the friendship of other women in ministry.

As I have worked beside my husband, I have often needed a friend on Monday mornings. Whether Sunday was thrilling or discouraging, the next day I would long for another woman to share my joys without jealousy and hear my frustrations without judgment. I was thankful for my two sisters and my mother, all ministry wives, who willingly played that role for me. Our Monday morning long-distance conversations were expensive, so somebody invented e-mail--just for us! Messages began to fly across the internet as we shared our hearts.

We were honest with each other. Perturbed by some tough circumstances, one of my sisters once sent me a note with this in the subject line: *Please delete after reading.* I sent back my own not long after that with this heading: *Please delete before reading.* If you can relate to that, you know what I mean when I say that once in a while we all need to unload to someone with skin on, someone who loves us enough to hear what we say with an understanding, empathetic heart.

When a pressured ministry friend asked if she could join our e-mail group, I said, "Sure—welcome to the Monday Morning Club!" And so began a circle of friends known by that name. This book is a compilation of regular e-mails sent all over the world to women in ministry who have asked to be part of the club.

Don't expect to find anything profound or eloquent here. These are just little letters to my friends. They span the decades from my early years as a pastor's wife with young children, to the years traveling with our growing family in itinerant evangelism, to our current ministry assisting church planters. As we spend time together, I hope you will know that I am your friend and that you are not alone.

You can read this book in the usual way, from start to finish, or open it at random and read whatever you happen upon. But on those days when you know exactly what you most need to hear, turn to the *Chapters by Topic* list to find notes on that subject written just for you, just for that morning. May the Lord use this book to help you keep pressing on!

1
New Haircut

I was nervous as I walked into the Wednesday night prayer service. I had a new and dramatically different haircut, one I knew people would notice. They did.

One of the first comments came from a leader in the church, a man whose approval I thought I needed. "Nice haircut," he said. "*Now* you look like a pastor's wife." I recognized this as a backhanded compliment, but I resisted the temptation to ask him what I had looked like before. Actually, I was pleased. Hooray for me, I thought. I got it right.

But the following Sunday morning, after I in my new hairdo confidently introduced myself to a visitor, she said, "*You're* the pastor's wife? I looked all around during the service and didn't see anybody I thought looked like a pastor's wife."

Oh, so maybe I didn't get it right. I managed to smile and once again withstood the urge to ask her to tell me what I did look like. Two people—two different images of some mythical creature called "The Pastor's Wife." I obviously couldn't please them both.

As I thought (and laughed) about it later, I realized that expectations for a pastor's wife go far beyond haircuts.

Every person in every pew has a job description for me, unwritten and usually unspoken, but real nevertheless. Two people? Two job descriptions. Two hundred people? Two hundred ideas of how I should look and what I should do. Obviously, I couldn't please them all. I decided to just try to please the Lord.

But what is His job description for me? I searched the New Testament and found in 1 Timothy 3 a list of qualifications for deacons' wives. But the only requirement for a pastor's wife is that there is to be only one of me. I can manage that.

Did the Holy Spirit forget my list? Did He run out of space before He got to it? Of course not. The message from that omission is clear. It encourages me, gives me peace, and sets me free.

The Lord's job description for me is simple: I am my husband's wife. Just like any other wife, I am a help meet for him—perfectly designed to be his partner in life and ministry. So I just ask my husband what I can do to help him and let him write my job description. He's the best one to do it, because he knows my skills, my energy level, and my season of life. And he loves me. Whenever I please him, I please the Lord.

So now when I get a new hairdo, I just ask my husband if he likes it. If he does—hooray for me! I got it right.

2
All Mine and All Yours, Too

The day had been long and demanding, but the sun was finally sinking, and I was cooking supper. I was kneading biscuit dough with one hand while balancing a cranky toddler on a hip with the other when the phone rang.

"Claudia, help! I don't know what to fix for dinner. My husband will be home any minute, and he's going to be really mad if nothing's cooking. What should I make?"

I recognized the voice of my friend. I had answered dozens of panicky calls like this from her—several earlier that day, in fact.

"Why is my washing machine making that weird noise?"

"Why do I feel so fat?"

"My kids are driving me crazy. Why won't they obey?"

"Our dog is barking and won't stop, and the neighbor says he's going to call the police. What should I do?"

She was a new believer, and I was her pastor's wife. I did want to help her, and she certainly needed it. Lots and lots and lots of help. But most of her problems had no simple solution, and her constant calls at inconvenient times were becoming annoying. I took a deep breath, and then another and another.

During the pause, I heard her say, "Oh, I just get so frustrated with you! You never have any problems. Why don't YOU ever have any problems?"

At that moment, my two daughters burst through the back door with tangled hair and dirty faces, one loudly complaining about some sort of backyard ruckus and the other whining that she was starving. The toddler in my arms lunged for the biscuit dough, crammed a floury handful into his mouth, gagged, and spewed it onto the floor. Rice boiled over on the stove, the front doorbell rang, and our car pulled into the driveway. My exhausted, hungry husband was coming home from a long day at church to a scene of minor domestic disaster.

So I did what every pastor's wife prays not to do: I said exactly what I was thinking. "No problems?" I blurted. "What do you mean? I have all my problems and all yours, too!"

The silence on the phone was even louder than the din in the kitchen. "Oh," my friend finally said, very quietly. "I guess you do."

And then to my enormous relief, she started to laugh. So did I. We laughed and laughed and laughed.

We remained friends, but never again was I up on her "pedestal of perfection." I was glad. I had never wanted to be there in the first place. I had never tried to portray myself as Mrs. Perfect, whose children always behaved and whose furniture never gathered dust; whose speech was always "with grace, seasoned with salt"; whose devotional life and daily discipline were models for all womankind.

But she had assumed that troubles wouldn't dare tiptoe through a parsonage door and that marrying a pastor somehow morphed an ordinary woman into a super saint who lived above the mundane.

I'm sure that in her own mind she was honoring me by placing me on a pedestal. That is, after all, where we put statues of people we admire. But it's not a comfortable place for a plain old human to live. It's lonely on a pedestal. Other people think you are looking down on them. There are pigeons. And if you stumble even once, you'll fall off.

Many church-pew-sitters share my friend's "pedestal of perfection" notion, however. That's why they are genuinely shocked when they discover that the pastor's wife has a flaw or two. Or why other more misguided folks delight in seeing her take a tumble down to where the real people live.

A ministry wife can't keep church folks from lifting her onto their imaginary pedestal. But she can avoid climbing up there herself. She can stop expecting perfection from herself or pretending it to others. The Lord only asks her to be the most Christlike woman she can be, crediting Him for her strengths, readily acknowledging her weaknesses, and quickly asking forgiveness for her failures.

Face the reality that in yourself you are nothing: "In me (that is, in my flesh) dwelleth no good thing" (Romans 7:18). Then remember that when He called you to ministry, He gave you the power and gifts needed for the job: "Not that we are sufficient of ourselves to think anything as of ourselves; but our sufficiency is of God" (2 Corinthians 3:5).

Maybe you will do your job so capably that there will someday be a statue of you—on a pedestal! But until then, remember that you are not made of marble. You are just yourself, a fallible female human given the blessed assignment of wife-ing a man in ministry. And despite what others may think, the job does not require living on a pedestal.

3
Mule Stuff

We love the Grand Canyon. On our family's first visit, after we had spent hours on the rim staring into its depths, we began a hike down into the canyon. Our children were young, so we didn't plan to go far. We chose the Kaibab Trail, which is also a path for the canyon's famous mule caravans.

After a few minutes, I heard a howl from one of our daughters. "Ugh! Yuck! Mule stuff!" She had discovered what the guidebooks don't mention: wherever there are mules, there are huge hunks of smelly droppings.

"Just step around it," came my husband's cheery voice. "Doesn't have to ruin our hike!" So on we went—Dad in front, children following, me bringing up the rear, watching the eight sneakered feet ahead of me as well as my own, imagining the long drive home closed up in our warm truck cab with five pairs of stinky shoes. I tromped down the trail, frowning at the thought of my malodorous future.

Suddenly I stopped in my tracks, feeling dumb. There I was in one of the most incredibly gorgeous places on earth, and I was ignoring the splendor all around me to focus on *manure*. How silly!

I stopped looking down and began to look up instead, and immediately my heart lifted. The Lord was in this place! His fingerprints were on every canyon wall. He, the Creator, had painted those remarkable hues. His voice echoed across the silence of the canyon's vast chasms right into my heart.

He told me that I had been living in the same way I was hiking—looking down, focusing on the negatives of the moment and dreading the future. I was allowing unhelpful people and painful problems to loom so large on my path that they blocked my vision of Him at work for me. Too often I could not, or would not, see past my own smelly discouragement to this splendid truth: the Lord is in every place.

Negatives come to ministry as frequently as mule caravans travel those canyon trails, and many days are littered with their droppings. But still the Lord is there. His hand is at work, transforming me through my trials, reminding me in gentle tones to trust Him to work *even this* together for my good. When I look down, I forget Him and get preoccupied with the ugly stuff along the path. When I look up, I remember Him and am helped.

The stinky mule stuff washed off our shoes just fine, even before we got back in the truck. Every minute I spent fretting was a waste of time I could have spent enjoying the scenery. We haven't hiked the Kaibab since, but I've never forgotten what I learned that day. I hope I never do.

4
Life on a Roller Coaster

Have you ridden on a roller coaster lately? If not, prepare yourself: there has been a roller coaster revolution. Those rides used to be predictable, with a few abrupt turns and several jerky, clickety climbs. After each ascent, you could expect a speedy but uncomplicated plunge. When the ride was over, you could deny that you had been terrified.

Not now. Allow yourself to be straitjacketed into one of the new breed of roller coasters, and you'll soon be upside-down more often than you are right-side-up. Don't be surprised to find yourself tunneling underground and hurtling up, down, around, and sideways at frightening speeds. And at the end of all that delightful fun, as you stagger away with your head spinning and your stomach lurching, you'll have the pleasure of seeing displayed on a big screen a thoroughly undignified shot of yourself mid-ride, hair on end, eyes wide, mouth screaming.

Yet you'll probably still hear yourself saying, "Wow—that was GREAT!" And it certainly was exhilarating. What made it pleasurable, though, or at least tolerable, was knowing that it would soon be over. Nobody wants a ride like that to last forever. If it went on for even one hour, what would happen? Desperate for escape, you might try to jump off.

You might get sick. You might die. Nobody can *live* on a roller coaster.

For too many of my early years as a ministry wife, that's where I lived—on an emotional roller coaster. My feelings swayed with whatever happened or didn't happen at church. I would be excited, discouraged, content, worried, elated, or miserable, depending on what had transpired on Sunday. I let the good and bad decisions of others control my emotions.

Negatives would plunge me into darkness, with a whirling mind and churning stomach. Positives sent me to an artificial high that was followed by the inevitable low. I couldn't sleep. My head hurt. I longed for stability and wondered how to get off the roller coaster before I died.

God sweetly began to teach me a life-changing lesson: He does not intend for me to live as a straitjacketed victim of my own volatile emotions. He doesn't want me to live on a roller coaster of my feelings but on the rock of this truth instead: my circumstances are directed by my wise Father. He plans and controls them. Good or bad, happy or sad, He has every one of them under control. And they are all for my good.

When you feel your coaster begin its dizzying roll, get out of there fast. Climb up to sit beside me on this solid rock: *"Thou wilt keep him in perfect peace whose mind is stayed on Thee, because he trusteth in Thee. Trust ye in the Lord forever, for in the Lord Jehovah is everlasting strength* [the Rock of Ages]" (Isaiah 26:3-4).

Have you been on an emotional roller coaster lately? Are you sick of it—literally? Get off that scary ride and stand on His promises instead.

10

5
Safety Latches

Getting our fifth-wheel home ready for travel is like getting ready for an earthquake. We have to roll up, take down, fold flat, or otherwise secure all our movable belongings. My final pre-travel checkpoint is always at the refrigerator. I close the door firmly, listening for the satisfying click that tells me it's shut tight. I'm obsessive about this, because I do not want a repeat of the Great Refrigerator Disaster.

The Disaster happened during a trip out west. The trailer we owned then had a removable safety latch on the refrigerator door which had to be taken out of a drawer and set in place before every move.

We left central California on a beautiful December morning and wound through the mountains a while before stopping for a break at the Casa de Coffee. Before going in, I quickly checked inside the trailer, where I discovered what I had forgotten: to set the safety latch.

The refrigerator had opened on a curve and hurled its contents onto the kitchen carpet. Heaped in a colorful mound were a quart of red spaghetti sauce, a dozen slimy yellow eggs, a gallon of creamy white milk, a pint of golden maple syrup, and several unrecognizable greenish, brownish, yellowish substances.

I cried, laughed, and cried again. We shoveled, scraped, and disposed of the mess. But that was not the end of it. The milk soured and stank for weeks. The spaghetti stain survived a barrage of carpet cleaners. The combination of sticky egg and gooey syrup left a patch of carpet permanently stiff.

That safety latch didn't look important. It was just a two-inch piece of black plastic. And neglecting to set it was only a tiny bit of forgetfulness. But that little mistake caused me hours of work, sour smells, stains, and frustration. I never could eradicate the reminders of my blunder. I reaped much more than I sowed.

The sowing of one small sin can bring any ministry wife a large, unwelcome harvest. One lie, one bit of gossip or lost temper, one impure act, one neglected duty, or one root of bitterness can lead to personal heartache and ministry difficulty. She may never be able to erase the scars or ease the effects. She can be fully forgiven but she may not ever fully recover.

Sounds discouraging, doesn't it? But the Lord our Helper is "touched with the feeling of our infirmities . . . in all points tempted like as we are, yet without sin." So every ministry wife can "come boldly unto the throne of grace, that [she] may obtain mercy, and find grace to help in time of need" (Hebrews 4:15-16).

If you only ask, the Lord will set His supernatural safety latches on your mouth, mind, and heart. Here are a couple to set every morning before you begin to travel through the day. As you pray them sincerely, He hears you, and you will hear a reassuring "click" every time He gives you power to resist temptation. Stay safe today.

"Let the words of my mouth, and the meditation of my heart, be acceptable in thy sight, O Lord, my strength, and my redeemer."
Psalm 19:14

"Set a watch, O Lord, before my mouth; keep the door of my lips. incline not my heart to any evil thing."
Psalm 141:3

6
Blue Blockers

My oversized sunglasses were scratched, wobbly, and terribly outdated when they finally died, but I was still sad to see them go. I am not usually sentimental about sunglasses, but after 15 years of faithful service, those "blue blocker" glasses were my special friends. Our children, for good reason, called them my happy glasses.

Through plain lenses, the world looked dull. Ugly, even. But through blue blockers, it was bright and beautiful. I don't know how they worked, though I think they filtered out some hues and enhanced others. I only know that when I wore them, ordinary flowers suddenly showed off gorgeous new tints. Autumn colors turned intense, and the sky was brighter than ever. Every sunset dazzled. I loved the way my blue blockers cheered otherwise dreary scenes.

The ministry world is not always lovely. We know that it is a privilege to serve the Lord, and we love working beside our husbands. But ministry is often tedious, and it may even turn ugly when we face frustration and failure. We accept this and endure.

But you and I can do more than just hang on and try to survive. If we can learn to look at ministry trials through the blue blockers of promise, we can thrive.

The first time I tried this was with an annoying church member. When I grumbled about him, my pastor husband suggested that he might actually be a gift from the Lord for my good, for he was my opportunity to practice loving the unlovely. If, my husband said, I would try to see him in that light, I'd find myself growing in the love of Christ. So I began looking at this man through the blue blocker truth that even *he* was God's gift for my good--and sure enough, his looks improved dramatically!

There is a specific promise for every ministry problem. When you encounter a financial shortfall, looking at it through the blue blocker of "God shall supply all your need" (Philippians 4:19) will help you to see it as an opportunity for the Lord to keep His promise to provide.

When you confront an impossible task, face it through the lens of "My strength is made perfect in weakness . . . for when I am weak, then am I strong" (2 Corinthians 12:10), and you will see it as an occasion for God to display His power at work in you.

Are you being persecuted for doing right? Then "rejoice and be exceeding glad, for great is your reward in heaven" (Matthew 5:12). Have you endured a humiliating failure? See it through the encouraging lens of "God resisteth the proud, but gives grace unto the humble" (James 4:6). Are you lonely? See in your loneliness a precious opportunity to draw near to God, to enjoy the fellowship of the Friend Who is closer than a brother.

When a scary ministry trial looms on your path, you have two choices. You can peek at it timidly through the lenses of your emotions and tremble. Or you can boldly stare through the lenses of truth and be joyful and brave. You already own a lifetime supply of blue blocking promises. No matter how old they get, they are never out of style. Each morning, pick out the ones you need for that day. Wear them all day long, and I suspect you'll find your world a much more beautiful place.

7
The Princess and the Pea

Do you remember that fairytale? The prince knew he had finally found a "real" princess to marry when she complained about her miserable night spent tossing and turning in her bed. Not even ten mattresses and ten featherbeds could cushion her delicate body from a single pea the queen had placed under them as a test. (Must have been a raw pea.)

As far as I know, I have never slept on a pea, cooked or uncooked. Or on ten mattresses and ten featherbeds, for that matter. But I have tossed and turned my way through some sleepless nights.

I sleep best when all my cushions are in place. I'm healthy. We are having visible ministry success. Our children are thriving. My husband says out loud that he thinks I'm a perfect wife. Friends speak well of me and my enemies are keeping quiet. I'm hearing more compliments than complaints. Our wallets are just fat enough. The house is reasonably clean and the calendar of events is manageable. At times like that, I sink into the pillows of prosperity and snooze away.

But sometimes the Lord takes them away and hands me sickness, family difficulties, and church conflicts instead. He takes away the featherbeds of comfortable friendships and allows financial strains and arduous schedules to steal my serenity. As my mattresses disappear one by one, I sink lower and lower, not only into restless nights, but even into doubt. Where is the Lord? Does He know? Does He care? And what has He done with my pillows?

When I finally hit bottom, I discover that I'm on a rock. The Solid Rock. I settle down and rest there in absolute tranquility as the God of *all* peace reminds me that He is the God of *my* peace. He is what I need — not all those cushions. I could never learn that, if He didn't now and then bring me to a place where I have to rest on the firm ground of His love alone.

God has been gracious to allow me, most of my life, to enjoy many of the comforts that make life pleasant. I must remember, though, that ten mattresses and ten featherbeds make an awfully wobbly bed. Circumstances are fleeting and unreliable, but He is my ever-present Rock. And when I am resting on Him alone, my sleep is sweet.

8
You Might Be a Pastor's Wife If . . .

You're at every church service—second row, piano side. You don't sit with your husband. He doesn't sit at all.

You arrive early and leave late, even if you have a headache or company. Or both.

You bring music for an emergency offertory and impromptu solo, just in case.

You turn off the coffeepot, dump the nursery diapers, and water the lobby ferns.

You starch white shirts and press gray suits.

When your husband buys a small red car, you fret that he won't look dignified driving in a funeral procession.

When your weary family needs to sleep late, you get up early, quietly dress, and put on makeup before lying down again, just in case that deacon happens to drop by. Then you can answer the door looking sort of okay and he won't tell people you are all lazy.

You're an expert at multiplying recipes to feed 12, 24, 48, or 96.

You keep a large aluminum pan of lasagna in the freezer, just in case.

You are able to give sincere thanks to the giver of *another* sack of zucchini.

To church fellowships, you bring loaves of zucchini bread.

You wince but don't panic when the phone rings early on Sunday morning. You've already prepared a Sunday school lesson, just in case.

You laugh at your husband's pulpit jokes before he gets to the punch lines and turn to the sermon text before it's announced.

Prayer requests and announcements prompt additions to the to-do list you've scribbled on the bulletin.

You notice new hairdos, new dresses, and which lady needs a hug. You provide compliments and hugs just in case no one else does.

You remember the names of grandchildren and new puppies.

You are able to smile sweetly at *another* family who say they will be out of town next Sunday and sincerely wish them a pleasant trip.

To attendance figures, you add the people who would have been there if they could have been there and come up with a new total just for yourself and your husband. You do this in the car on the way home.

You work beside your husband without schedule, salary, or job description. You love your job. Usually.

You may already know how valuable you are. Maybe your congregation praises you openly and often. I hope so. But, just in case, let me assure you: your church is stronger because of you. You are its caregiver and its sparkle. Its wheels roll more smoothly because you sweep the pebbles out of its path. Without you, your husband's task would be harder. And the lobby ferns would die.

Look in the mirror and smile. You have chosen a career with both earthly value and eternal significance, and you are doing a great job. Hooray for you—you're a pastor's wife!

9
Grandmaville

I have recently moved to Grandmaville. An adorable grandson occupies this new town with me. I am content here, for I have found that Grandmaville has many advantages over Mothertown.

I feed that grandboy cookies. Someone else will teach him to swallow squash. I rock him and sing lullabies, but someone else does it in the middle of the night. He crawls onto my lap to hear a story, but his real education is someone else's job. I admire the Sunday suit that someone else has to pay for and keep clean. I stop him from running into traffic, but the ultimate responsibility for his physical and moral safety rests on someone else's shoulders.

I enjoy being his friend. I teach him what I can, set an example for him, pray for him, and love him, but his parents are ultimately accountable for him — not me. That is liberating! The freedom to treasure this child without bearing the essential burdens of meeting his needs and controlling his behavior makes Grandmaville a peaceful place. I sleep well, knowing he is in good hands.

My grandson is someone else's child. So is that person in the pew for whom you feel so responsible. If she has been born into God's family, she is His child. He has charged Himself with her welfare. He watches over her, meets her needs, protects her from danger, and comforts her in trouble. "Like as a father pitieth his children, so the Lord pitieth them that fear Him" (Psalm 103:13). He gladly bears full responsibility for her well-being.

And He knows when His child does wrong. He will discipline, "for whom the Lord loveth He chasteneth, and scourgeth every son whom He receiveth . . . for what son is he whom the father chasteneth not?" (Hebrews 12:6). Our children sometimes choose to disobey. They go astray and break our hearts. So do His children. And just like any diligent parent, our Heavenly Father loves, woos, and seeks to draw His rebellious children back into the family fold.

Because we have the mothering instinct, ministry wives are prone to think of the people in the pews as our children. We believe that we are responsible for them. And in a sense, we are. Paul spoke for us in Colossians 1:28: "We preach, warning every man, and teaching every man in all wisdom; that we may present every man perfect in Christ Jesus, whereunto I also labor . . . . "

So as we get to know "our" people, we work hard to meet their needs, physical and emotional as well as spiritual. We make their burdens our own, even the ones we have no way to lighten. We do this because we love them, but as we do, we sometimes make them dependent on us rather than on their real Father.

When they do wrong, we feel as personally responsible to ensure their repentance and restoration as we would feel for our own disobedient children. But often they won't listen and won't do right. They won't be drawn back even by our most heartfelt pleas. So we lie awake, weeping and worrying over "our" wayward children, thinking that it's our job to — somehow — *make* them do right.

That's when we need to recall this important fact: they are Someone Else's children! The Omniscient God knows their needs and will provide. His eyes "run to and fro throughout the whole earth" (2 Chronicles 16:9), seeing the same sins we see and many more besides. He knows how to discipline His children, and He will do it, even without our help.

Come live with me in Grandmaville. It's nice here. Enjoy His children. Be their friend. Teach them what you can, set an example for them, pray for them, and love them. But relax, remembering that they are ultimately His, and He is capable of taking care of them. They are in His good hands.

10
Traveling Together

David and I were making yet another coast-to-coast drive together, this time from South Carolina to California. Well, we weren't exactly *together*, since he pulled our fifth-wheel trailer with our diesel pickup while I followed in our cozy and comfortable car. We made up our own short parade. Day after day, as America the Beautiful rolled by, I steered and stared and reflected. By the time we reached San Diego, I had figured this out: our duo driving was very much like our ministry marriage ought to be.

It was an easier drive for me than for my husband. Every morning we huddled over the atlas and agreed on our route. Then all I had to do was follow. I didn't have to consult the map, watch for the next exit, or check my speed. He broke the trail and set the pace. He deflected the wind and the bugs. I just had to stay close behind and steer straight. When I thought he might be making a mistake, I mentioned it, but even when he made a wrong turn, I followed. (He didn't make many.)

We communicated constantly with old-fashioned walkie-talkies. We pointed out the beauty of the desert sunrise and warned each other of dangers like wrecks and weird drivers. We laughed at the cloud of feathers swirling around a chicken truck. We made up stupid jokes.

To communicate, we had to stay close. When we drifted apart, our words were broken by static and were easy to misunderstand. Too many cars between us created interference, so we stayed close together, especially in heavy traffic.

We checked on each other frequently: "Need fuel? Coffee? Chocolate? Are you sleepy? Hungry? Bored?" When either of us had a need, we both stopped, and we didn't press on until we were both ready to go. Rest stops were crucial. They kept us awake and helped us reconnect. We each felt responsible for the other's well-being. We wanted to reach the day's goal, but only if we reached it safely and together.

The roads were usually smooth, but some had potholes. Most days were sunny, but a few were foggy or stormy. Crosswinds occasionally threatened to push us off the pavement, but more often, soft breezes drifted through our open windows.

Whatever the condition of the asphalt or the weather, though, we stayed on the right road. We couldn't control the weather or improve the condition of the highway. We were only responsible for driving as carefully as we could in the right direction and for staying together.

Whether you're traveling across the country or down a ministry road, you're safer together than alone. It's more interesting and lots more fun. But it's also more work, for there are threats to our togetherness. Bumpy pavement, busy traffic, and poor weather pull us apart and hinder our communication. They tempt us to think more about the potholes and gloomy skies than each other. We may thoughtlessly forge ahead with ministry without taking time for rest stops or to take care of each other's needs. If we don't agree on our route or both try to lead, we may end up traveling in opposite directions and lose each other completely.

Two people, two vehicles, but one unit—that was us on our cross-country trek. Praise the Lord, we arrived unharmed on the other shore. May you and your husband arrive safely, too.

11
A Little Pot

A little pot sits alongside the other pots in my kitchen cabinet. It's dented and discolored. It doesn't have an insulated handle or even a lid to call its own. Too small for most cooking tasks, it has spent most of its life sitting in the shadows looking insignificant.

This little pot has an inglorious past—my husband the dumpster diver rescued it from someone else's trash. After I cleaned it up, I discovered that although ugly, that pot was a genius at one thing: boiling water. For a cup of hot tea, it's even faster than the microwave, and though it holds only two eggs, it boils them in record time. For the last 40 years, it's been my reliable friend.

I hope my odd little pot has never felt inferior to the shinier, fancier occupants of my kitchen. But if it does, I understand, for I'm terribly prone to compare myself to others and find myself wanting.

Maybe you, too, measure yourself against others. That other woman can sing in a way that moves hearts, but you can't. Not by a long shot! Another one has a glorious salvation testimony that moves women to tears, but yours is sort of boring. Then there's the one who can play any song on the piano in any key at any time, beautifully. Not you.

That one sparkles and bubbles. She dazzles! You, on the other hand, are reserved by nature. She glides through social events with ease. You'd rather hide in a corner. She's prettier, thinner, and smarter than you. Her spiritual gifts have opened doors to a public role in a ministry where she is celebrated and honored, but you serve in an anonymous place to little acclaim.

You may picture her as a gleaming, non-stick, copper-clad pot in the Lord's kitchen and imagine yourself as an odd pot of small worth. But the Lord does not see you that way at all, for you are custom-designed for His purpose, "fearfully and wonderfully made" (Psalm 139:14). He has assigned tasks to you that you can do better than anyone else in the world.

Imagine a kitchen where all the pots were exactly alike. If they were all crockpots, the cook couldn't fry chicken. If they were all skillets, making potato soup would be awfully hard. A cook needs a variety of tools, each designed for a specific purpose. And the Lord needs a diverse group of women for ministry, each uniquely equipped for His intended use.

If I were to put my funny little pot in a rummage sale, it wouldn't sell, even for a quarter. But it will never be for sale, because I value it. I need it just as it is. And the Lord needs a woman just exactly like you.

12

Questioning the Lord

A ministry wife was talking to her Lord.

She said:
Lord, why aren't people faithful to church? They make such silly excuses to stay away.
He answered:
I understand. This morning I waited for you at our usual meeting place, but you didn't come. Did you have something more important to do?

She said:
Lord, people let us down. They promise to do a task and then they don't do it. Why don't they honor their commitments?
He answered:
People are like that. By the way, do you remember those vows you once made to Me?

She said:
Lord, the people we serve rarely say thanks. We aren't appreciated.
He answered:
I make My sun rise on the evil and on the good. I send rain on the just and the unjust. And I daily load you down with benefits. Have you noticed?

She said:
Lord, we helped that family! We won them to You and discipled them, but now they have rejected us and joined another church. Loving people is just too painful. I quit.
He answered:
I understand. Many of My disciples went away and walked no more with Me. Will you also go away?

She said:
Lord, I'm homesick. Why can't I serve You closer to home?
He answered:
I came to earth from heaven, not to do My own will but the will of Him that sent Me. Whose will do you want to do?

She said:
Lord, we can't afford to buy nice things like our church members have. It isn't fair for us to work so hard and earn so little.
He answered:
The foxes have holes and the birds of the air have nests; but I had nowhere to lay My head. I became poor so that through My poverty you might become rich. Will you follow Me?

She said:
Lord, we faithfully give people the gospel, but they don't listen. Sometimes they even laugh at us.
He answered:
The servant is not greater than her Lord. If they have persecuted Me, they will persecute you. They do these things to you for My name's sake. Will you be crucified with Me?

She said:
Lord, I can't do this job. It's too hard.
He answered:
My grace is enough for you. My strength is made perfect in your weakness. When you are weak, then you are strong. Will you glory in your infirmities, so My power can rest on you?

She said:
Lord, make me like You.
He answered:
That's what I've been trying to do. Are you ready now?

13
Roosters

We have parked our trailer in many beautiful places--by rocky streams and on grassy hillsides, in deer-filled woods and by tranquil lakes. But other sites have been more—well, more interesting.

We spent a while living under the flight path for airliners heading overseas from a Chicago airport. Gigantic and heavy with passengers, baggage, and fuel, they skimmed the trees and our trailer home, so low we could see the bolts in the landing gear. In Atlanta, we were close enough to a train track to wave to the engineers from bed. We have often had horses, cows, and cornstalks as neighbors.

Our most memorable neighbors by far, however, were The Roosters. They lived next door—18 of them, each with its own wire cage, but no hens in sight. They were proud and colorful, with elaborate combs and tails. And they were talented. They could sing!

I'm a city girl. I had the notion that each farm had one rooster who flapped quietly to the top rail of a white fence at sunrise and gave one polite crow to inform the farmer that it was time to rise and shine. I don't know what I thought the rooster did next. Went back to bed for a while, I suppose.

These roosters did no such thing. They crowed in the dark, in the light, and in the rain. They sang duets, trios, quartets, and competed for the loudest and longest crow. For a day or two we slept with pillows over our ears and wondered where to find a recipe for rooster stew.

But then something changed. We got used to the noise. Occasionally we would notice an especially shrill crow, but soon we were able to ignore the racket enough to sleep through the night and in general were no longer disturbed by it.

People are adaptable. Whatever we see or hear enough times will start to seem normal. Hearing a lie often enough may be all it takes to convince us that it is true. Seeing Wrong for a long enough time, we may come to believe that it is actually Right. That is why we ought to stay far away from sin. After enough exposure time, we may start to see the abnormal as normal. Habit can make evil seem like good.

I didn't have a choice about living next door to the Roosters, so I had to get used to them. My ears went numb. But I do have a choice about living too close to sin. May I never get used to it. May my moral sense never go numb.

14
Dependability

We count on our little fan to sing us to sleep every night. It hides near the bed all day and goes to work when we are ready to snooze. Its gentle hum has just enough volume to block most outdoor sounds (which for us change often). Without this white noise, we'd wake up a dozen times a night. With it, we sleep in peace to a sweet fan lullaby.

Our little fan friend doesn't seem to want or need much attention. But once in a while, when too much dust accumulates on its insides, it goes on strike. It overheats and refuses to spin. No more lullaby. No more sleep. It won't hum again until we have vacuumed away the dirt. When it's clean, it's dependable. When it's dirty, it isn't. Simple as that.

I am not a fan or machine of any kind, and neither are you. But women in ministry operate in much the same way as that fan. There are people counting on us—husbands and children and church folks among them. We are nearly always where we are expected to be, doing what we're supposed to be doing, and smiling besides.

But sometimes we don't feel like doing our job right or even doing it at all. We'd rather not be patient and loving at home and kind, energetic, and creative at church. We want to hide someplace and take care of our own needs instead. Our hearts, if not our bodies, go on strike.

When that happens, it's a sure sign that the dust of self has clogged our works, and we need a heavenly clean-up. We won't be useful again until we are washed with His precious blood. Once that's happened, His Spirit begins to fill our emptiness, His love channels through us, and His power energizes us. What a difference! We get back to work, and we even start smiling again.

When we're clean, you can count on us. When we're not, you can't. Simple as that!

15
The Ocean

Ah-h-h-h—the salty sea! We love it. We have a family collection of happy ocean memories: pelicans in South Carolina, sea lions in Argentina, crystal sand along the Gulf of Mexico, jagged cliffs at Big Sur. We've never met an ocean we didn't like.

But sometimes I wonder why, since so many inconveniences and irritations come with life at the seashore. The sand that feels so warm and soft between our bare toes on the beach comes home with us as an uninvited and unwelcome guest. We shake it out of shoes, towels, and sheets. We crunch it along with the lettuce on our ham sand-wiches.

The sun which paints the sky that glorious blue and sprinkles glitter on the waves also stings our shoulders and raises blisters on our noses. The salty breeze that lifts our kites and refreshes our musty lungs also piles our hair into gummy haystacks. We wade in gently lapping waves, but under those soft swells hide jellyfish that sting and crabs that pinch.

We know that on every ocean holiday we'll be stung and pinched and burned and uglified, but we're still drawn like magnets to the seashore. We treat the irritations as trivialities, as the small price we pay for the privilege of enjoying the glories of the ocean. We take the bad with the good, minimize the one and maximize the other. We've decided that the beach is worth it.

And so is the ministry. When we stop to count our blessings, any difficulty that is native to serving the Lord becomes as insignificant as a sand burr stuck in a toe.

What could be better than being married to a man who would rather study and preach God's Word than peddle widgets? What's sweeter than the hug of a lady you've just led to Christ? Who could be more precious than the children in your Sunday school class? What would you rather do than invest your brief life in a cause that is guaranteed to ultimately succeed? What better employer than the King of Kings?

Your daily routine has eternal significance just because you are in the ministry. The annoyances that come with it are just trivialities. Is the ministry worth it? Yes! Absolutely yes!

16

Thinking about You

"I'm thinking about you."

Those are sweet words for anyone to hear. But to a woman in ministry, they are more than pleasant. They are precious, for all day you give your time and energy to others and have little time (or inclination) to focus on yourself.

So when some perceptive friend says, "I'm thinking about you," those simple words lift your heart. They encourage you, for they mean that your needs are noticed, and that you are loved. But even a friend who is insightful enough to see your needs may be unable to meet them. Thinking is all she can do.

God thinks about you, too. Do you know how often? Psalm 139:17-18 gives the answer: "How precious also are Thy thoughts unto me, O God! How great is the sum of them! If I should count them, they are more in number than the sand; when I awake, I am still with Thee."

When our son Jeremiah was little, we read Psalm 139:18 together, and then he asked me, "How many is that?"

"How many is what?" I responded.

"How many is the number of the sand?"

"It's a lot," I assured him, ready to move on to the next verse.

"Can we count them?" he persisted.

"Well, we could count some," I agreed, deciding that it would be good math practice. We filled a cup with sand and used a toothpick, a sheet of white paper, and a magnifying glass to count the grains.

I quickly realized that this would take more time than I had and larger numbers than he knew, so I suggested that we count just one spoonful. Still there were far too many, so we decided to count only the grains of sand that stuck to one of his little fingers and then were brushed onto the paper.

"42!" he exclaimed as he finished. "Wow—did God think about me 42 times today?"

Every day, the God of the universe is thinking about you. Even if you could number every grain of sand on the earth, you still would not know how often He does, for His thoughts are "more in number than the sand." Our counting skills are finite; His thoughts are infinite.

And His thoughts aren't just numerous. They are constant. You are never out of your Father's mind. This psalm says that He knows when you sit, when you stand, what you think, where you go, what you say—"all your ways." He never turns His eyes or His thoughts from you.

He has a special reason for thinking about you this much: He has given His word that He will take care of you. God doesn't only know your needs; He meets them—every one of them. His hand leads you and His right hand holds you. He protects you and provides for you.

So spend today as you usually do, meeting the needs of others. Don't worry about your own needs. They'll all be taken care of. Your Father is thinking about you.

17
Strawberries

Are the strawberries ripe where you live? One morning as I sampled berries at a farmer's market, memories flooded my mind of summer mornings and strawberry jam.

I would roll out of bed early and drive to the U-Pick farm. As the sun rose, I filled baskets with berries, lifting green leaves to discover the bright red fruit hiding in their shade. Every one seemed like a treasure. I drove home with the overflowing baskets cradled on the back seat so they wouldn't get bruised, smiling despite my aching back and stained knees.

At home I set the berries on the kitchen counter to be admired. Always, always, our family declared them the best ones ever. We sliced the sweet fruit into our breakfast cereal and savored every bite.

Then I went to work. First I dumped the berries into the sink and drowned them in icy water. Then I pulled off their green wigs and sliced them with a sharp knife. I crushed them, boiled them, ladled them into jars, sealed them, and boiled them again.

Poor little berries. I'm sure they were bewildered. After treating them as beloved treasures, I brought them pain and misery. But I knew it was necessary if I wanted to preserve them. Without the crushing and cooking, they would rot. Unless I smashed them into jam, they would not be useful.

Suppose one cute berry saw what was coming her way and decided to run from the pain. While my back was turned, she scrambled out of her basket and rolled across the kitchen counter to cower under the toaster oven. She hid there in the darkness, cringing while her berry friends met their awful fate. A week later, when I moved the toaster oven to wipe up crumbs, what would I find?

One rotten strawberry. Useless. Doomed to a gruesome death in the garbage disposal. The poor thing didn't understand the purpose of the process. I wasn't tormenting those berries. I was preparing them to be useful, to be a blessing to my family during the long winter ahead. I wish she had trusted and yielded to me, the wise maker of jam, who could see her future.

Sometimes when the Lord sends pain, I run away from it. I tremble and cry, "What's going on? What are You doing? I thought You said You loved me. I thought You said I was precious to You. Why are You treating me like this?"

But suffering has a purpose. Through it, He is making us useful, preparing us to be a sweet blessing to others in their winter seasons. He is preserving us in His own precious likeness.

So if right now you are being cut, crushed, and smashed by your circumstances, it's because He loves you enough not to let you mold and rot. He has plans for you, so yield to Him. The wise Almighty Creator sees your future, and He knows what He's doing.

18
Chocolate Pie

Our daughter was soon to be married, and she was determined to learn to make the chocolate pies her husband-to-be loved. We were delighted to let her practice on us over and over again. But one day as she was nearing pie perfection, ugly lumps appeared in her creamy filling.

"Mom, help! What can I do?" she asked.

I was scurrying around, busy with other things, but I paused long enough to suggest, "Pour it through the colander to strain out the lumps, and it will be fine."

So just as she had often seen me drain water from a pot of boiled pasta, she set the colander in the kitchen sink and poured the lumpy filling through the strainer--right down the drain. I found her standing by the sink with an odd look on her face, staring down into the colander, which held a small heap of still-steaming chocolate lumps—and nothing else.

She was embarrassed and unhappy, but she quickly recovered and cooked up another batch of her fabulous filling. Now she is a proficient cook, and her chocolate pies are family-famous.

I have made my own share of blunders in and out of the kitchen. I have even been known to pour life's sweetness down the drain and save the lumps.

Some days are full of those icky lumps. People who promise to come to church don't come, and you feel let down. People who are thoughtless make critical remarks, and you are hurt. People who should be helpers become hindrances instead, and you are frustrated. People you've worked with and prayed for don't respond to your ministry, and you are discouraged. People who used to be faithful become careless, and you are disappointed. People with obligations neglect their duties, so you have to add their tasks to yours, and you are annoyed — and annoyed with yourself for being annoyed.

Ministry, so full of sweet blessings, inevitably holds some bitter lumps as well. The Lord allows them as a way for you to share in the fellowship of His sufferings. Don't be surprised when you run across a few lumps. Just don't pour the sweetness down the drain to focus on them.

For every person who doesn't show up at church services, there's surely at least one who does. Look at her and heartily praise the Lord! Turn up the volume on sweet compliments, and the sound of bitter complaints will fade. Call to mind the faces of responsive, dependable people, and the difficult, apathetic ones won't seem such a burden. Give frequent thanks for (and to) every sweet encourager and helper, and you won't be nearly so preoccupied with the lumpier folks.

One good thing about a kitchen disaster: the cook can always throw it away and start over. This may be the day for you to discard an old habit of focusing on the negatives and stir up a thankful, positive spirit instead. Throw away the lumps and enjoy the sweetness!

19

Greg

Greg was in his regular place on the front pew. Since he rarely missed a service, I was used to looking at the back of his head from my spot on the second pew.

He had started coming to our church just after it was planted. In those early days, he often walked several miles along a busy road to get to the building where we met. He'd come trudging along in overcoat and boots, big Bible under his arm, and he was usually early.

We built our first church building closer to his home, so his walk was much shorter to Sunday school, prayer meeting, choir practice, and everything else. He sang loudly, with the music held close to his face because even with thick lenses in his glasses, seeing to read was difficult. But he loved to sing. In fact, he loved everything about church.

Especially fellowship meals. He loaded his plate and went through the line several times. And children — he loved talking to them and giving them gifts. Evangelists who set up tape tables during revival meetings were happy to see him coming, because he would buy one of everything they had. He had a humble but well-paying job and enjoyed spending his money.

But occasionally other folks at church weren't thrilled that he was there. He laughed too loud. He monopolized visitors. He lacked social skills.

But what he didn't lack was love for the Lord. He had accepted Jesus as his Savior and had been baptized; he often asked for prayer for his mother, father, and brothers to be saved. He gave out tracts and invited people to church. He may not have understood much about theology, but he knew all he needed to know to be saved and to serve his Savior.

On the Sunday I remember best, I had watched him scribbling madly in a fat spiral notebook during the sermon. He had looked up at my husband occasionally, but for the most part he simply wrote as fast as he could. As soon as the service was over, I leaned forward to ask, "What are you writing in your notebook?"

He squinted at me through those thick lenses. "Sermon notes," he replied. "I can't understand all the preacher's words at first, so I write them down and then I go home and read them some more, and every time I read them, I figure them out a little better. That's what I'm doing."

Oh. I had been listening to the message, too. Well, I'm pretty sure I did. Maybe I had been thinking about another thing or two at the same time. Important thoughts, I assured myself, but I knew they weren't nearly as important as the truth being taught from the pulpit. Suddenly my own notes looked awfully skimpy.

I'm not so vain that I think I already know it all and don't have to listen to the preaching, but sometimes I act like it. Not Greg. He worked to understand every word. He was using much more of the ability God gave him than I was. If we're all just stewards of our gifts, I asked myself that morning, which of us was more faithful?

I wasn't happy with the obvious answer to my question. And I have never forgotten the Lord's living application to me of 1 Corinthians 4:7: "For who maketh thee to differ from another? And what hast thou that thou didst not receive? Now if thou didst receive it, why dost thou glory, as if thou hadst not received it?"

One day, we will all be the same—just like Christ. Until then, those who for a little while are a little different have something to teach the rest of us. He only asks us to be faithful stewards of our gifts. But He does ask that.

20
An Ordinary Day

An ordinary day – help me to realize what a treasure you are.

That slogan painted on a wooden sign caught my attention at a yard sale. I didn't buy the sign, but I have never forgotten the words.

They came to mind at the close of an ordinary day when the road was level and the scenery familiar. No catastrophes or crises broke the monotony. I faced no hurricanes, tornadoes, or earthquakes (meteorological or emotional). It was a commonplace day, with its regular routine and familiar cadence of housework and ministry. On this day, my sky didn't fall.

But neither did my road rise to meet the skies. Without any bright joys or scary surprises, the day seemed flat. Dull, even. It was a ho-hum, same old-same old day. At bedtime I could have written in my journal, "Nothing happened today."

But how wrong I would be. On this ordinary day, I served the King of Kings! My mundane chores were His assignments. When I cut out flannelgraph pictures and folded bulletins, I did His work. When I washed dishes and children's faces, I washed His feet. He once carried a towel to reveal the glory of faithfulness in the ordinary. Today's simple tasks were menial, but they were not insignificant.

And also on this most ordinary of days, the King took care of me. He Who "knows my downsitting and my uprising . . . my path and my lying down," Who is "acquainted with all my ways," hedged me in on every side, all day long (Psalm 139). Wherever I went, I was secure in His strong right hand. He re-routed tempests and held my sky in place. He shielded me from virulent viruses, enraged enemies, and drunk drivers. On this quiet day, I can gather my wits and calm my heart, for tomorrow I may have to face dreadful perils. How good He is to give me this ordinary day.

But maybe there's no such thing as an ordinary day — for every day that the God of the universe lets me serve Him, every day that I enjoy His unseen, providential care, is an amazing gift of divine love.

Have an extraordinary, ordinary day!

21
A Clean Kitchen

I'm not sure why I was sitting on the kitchen floor that Monday morning. I think it had something to do with the dog. But there I was, nose to nose with Max, who was a very short dog. I looked around and was appalled at what I saw. Morsels of dried-up food in dark recesses. (Why didn't you eat those, Max?) Splatters of milk and grease on cabinet doors. Splotches of (what is that?) on the floor by the stove. A few dead flies. And that greasy grunge along the edge of the refrigerator — yuck.

Yesterday when company was here for dinner, this kitchen was clean! At least I thought it was. It had looked clean when my eyes were up at head level where they usually are. I distinctly remembered my pride in its shininess. This pastor's wife could manage it all, I had thought. Even on Sunday, she glides with ease through duties both public and domestic.

How smug I was. And how fortunate that yesterday's guests were too dignified to inspect my kitchen's grubby crannies. Or maybe they had noticed and were too polite to mention it. This kitchen wasn't clean at all. It was sparkling on the surface but grimy underneath.

I was tempted to ignore the covert dirt. If nobody else knew about it, I could just pretend I didn't either. But my housewifely conscience soon conquered my laziness. I pulled on plastic gloves, grabbed a rag and a strong cleanser, and attacked. It wasn't a quick or pleasant job, but it was satisfying. Soon the kitchen was genuinely clean. The hidden crud was gone. No one else may ever have noticed, but that didn't matter. Max and I knew, and that was enough.

Memories of that morning came to me recently as I studied Psalm 51, David's psalm of private repentance. "Wash me completely, thoroughly, fully," he begged the Lord. "Eradicate my sin. Cleanse me with hyssop, like a leper is cleansed. Purify my inward, hidden parts. Make my heart as white as snow."

David was not satisfied with outward show. He wanted personal purity. It was not enough for him to look kingly; he longed for inward righteousness. Nowhere in his prayer-song did he ask God to restore his reputation or the respect of his court. He just wanted to be right with God.

As I read, I wondered: do I care more about what church folks think of me than about what God knows me to be? Do I sit smugly, self-righteously, in my queenly pastor's-wife-pew week after week, hoping that all those wicked sinners listening to my husband's sermon will get right with God? Why I am so seldom found kneeling in repentance during the invitation? (What would people think?) Am I complacent about my sin as long as I believe nobody else knows? Am I only superficially righteous?

Those questions sent me to my knees. The Lord and I peered into the grubby crannies of my heart, and He exposed the grime of secret sin. Once I saw it, there was no time for lazy apathy. It called for the immediate application of Christ's cleansing blood instead.

The problem with cleaning the kitchen is that it gets dirty again in a hurry. It's about time for another on-the-kitchen-floor dirt hunt. Come help me, and then we'll have dinner! But as for my heart— that's a private, daily cleaning project that keeps me on my knees. You may not ever notice, but God and I know, and that's enough.

22
A Comfortable Life

Where did that lady go—the one you used to be? Do you remember her?

She had a comfortable life. She slept late on Saturdays, and Sundays were restful. She got to church just as the service started and left when it was over. She usually sat with the same best friend. When she was sick, she stayed home. She noticed bulletin typos but felt no responsibility for them. She once brazenly wore new clothes to church two Sundays in a row. She focused on worship without counting absentees and stayed in her pew throughout entire Christmas programs.

She answered her door in robe and curlers. She hung underwear on the backyard clothesline. She ran to the grocery store without makeup. She fearlessly donated to the thrift store tacky gifts from church folks. She went on vacation without combining the trip with a seminar and relaxed without worrying that someone would die while she was out of town.

She had a first name then, but now she's Mrs. Pastor and The Church Hostess and The Teacher and The Luncheon Planner and Their Mother and The Visitor of All Visitors and Mrs. Many Other Responsibilities. Her new titles have brought with them perpetual burdens. She's tired and a little frustrated; sometimes she longs to trade places with her former self, to be unfettered from others' great expectations and complicated needs.

This morning, does your ministry weigh heavy? Are you longing for some easier way to make a living? Most of us do at some point, because ministry is not painless. Serving others is complicated, stressful, and draining. But in the most essential way, it's the best life of all, for it's a life that shapes us into the image of Christ.

The Christlike life has nothing at all to do with satisfying, coddling, or promoting self, but everything to do with being poured out for others. It calls for surrendering pleasures and yielding rights just as Christ "being in the form of God, thought it not robbery to be equal with God, but made Himself of no reputation, and took upon Him the form of a servant" (Philippians 2:6-7). More than any other vocation, ministry offers the privilege of exchanging self-gratification for self-expenditure — of becoming like the One Who "pleased not Himself" (Romans 15:3).

So cheerily wave goodbye to that other lady with her comfortable life. She's probably jealous of you, anyway — for you're beginning to look a lot like Him.

23
The High Wire

I sat in the grandstand, neck craned as I watched a famous circus family perform on a high wire. They all executed extraordinary feats of balance, but I, who find it difficult to walk and talk simultaneously, was especially intrigued with one female member of the troupe.

It was her name, not her acrobatics, that caught my attention. The rest of the family had exotic European names, but hers was the ordinary American name "Debbie". She looked different from the others, too, but her strength and grace matched theirs. She never lost her poise on the wire, never even seemed hesitant. I decided that she must have been born into another circus family and married into this one. With inherited circus genes and inbred talent, I thought, she probably took her first steps on a high wire.

I was right about the married-into part, but wrong about the rest. Debbie, I discovered, was once an earthbound mortal like me, a journalist who had interviewed one of the family sons, fallen in love, and married him and his circus life. Motivated by love, she had conquered her fears and learned to be an acrobat. Now she performed confidently on the high wire, with many years of practice disguised as natural talent.

The top of a circus tent is not God's place for me. I am very sure He wants me on the ground. But I've often felt like a Debbie on a high wire, called to tasks for which I have no natural ability, simply because I married my husband. I've quivered at my public duties and trembled at my private ones. I know my innate fears and natural weaknesses. I acknowledge my imperfections. How easily I could fall—and how much is at stake if I do!

The Lord has rarely given me a task for which I felt I had inherent aptitude. Maybe it's the same for you. If so, remember this—His strength lies precisely at the point of your weakness (2 Corinthians 12:10). Climb up on that scary high wire because you love Him, and do His will. You'll find yourself abundantly supplied with grace disguised as talent.

The Lord specializes in taking ordinary Debbies and using them in extraordinary ways. He doesn't ask you to do what's easy, but only what He enables, for then He is the One Who receives glory, especially from that lady up on the high wire.

24
Plugging In

I was preparing a hurry-up Sunday meal. Spaghetti sauce was bubbling in the crockpot, salad had been tossed into bowls, the oven was preheating for crusty bread, and the water for pasta was—well, it was supposed to be boiling on the front burner of the stove. It was certainly taking its own sweet time, I grumbled as I peeked under the lid.

I sliced, buttered, and slid the garlic bread into the oven and checked again. Still no bubbles; nothing was happening. "Boil, pot!" I demanded in frustration, and waited a few more minutes. Not even a simmer. I decided that that stovetop burner must have given up the ghost.

But as I investigated, I found out that the problem wasn't with the stove; it was with me. I had never turned it on. Poor cold pot. There was no flame, and she couldn't work up a boil all by herself, no matter how hard she tried.

Then I felt sorry for her. I was making demands on her that she could never fulfill. A few hours earlier, I had sat in my Sunday pew like a pot on a cold stove. My inner fire had gone away, and my joy with it. Rather than being "fervent in spirit, serving the Lord," I was listless and apathetic, going through the motions of ministry. I had held myself aloof from people who needed my warmth because I knew I had none to give. I had dragged myself stiffly through the duties of the morning, wondering miserably what had blown out my flame.

While gazing at that cold pasta pot, I figured it out. I had been trying to generate fervent, passionate service all by myself. In the morning rush, I had not taken time to plug into my outside power: the Holy Spirit, the only source of spiritual energy. Without a steady connection to Him, I was doomed to labor through ministry chores with half a cold heart.

The Holy Spirit had not left me. He was as close as my Bible. As soon as I could, I opened it, and He promptly pointed me to truths that defrosted my spirit. I unbolted the doors of my cold heart, and He cleansed and warmed chilly rooms that my sin had closed off to Him.

Once I turned the right knob on high, the pasta pot began bubbling cheerfully. And once the Holy Spirit had re-ignited my spirit, I was no longer just a stiff shell of a servant. He quickly thawed my heart, and before the Sunday evening service, He had proved this promise true: "And God is able to make all grace abound toward you; that ye, always having all sufficiency in all things, may abound [boil over] to every good work" (2 Corinthians 9:8).

25
The Looney Reunion

A small sign stood by the road in rural Tennessee. "Looney Reunion," it said, and below was an arrow pointing the way. I wondered—if I followed that arrow, would I arrive not at a family reunion, but at a gathering of ministry wives?

It's easy to get to the Looney Reunion. Just follow these directions.

ALWAYS
Sit in the back so you can watch people's reactions to your husband in the pulpit.
Count absentees rather than blessings.
Entertain formally in a spotless house, using complicated recipes, linen napkins, your wedding china, and Grandma's lace tablecloth.
Expect your children to behave like short grown-ups.
Wonder "what she meant by that."
When you are sick, be in the pew instead of in the bed.
Do at least three things at once.

NEVER
Forgive.
Delegate.
Sleep late.
Develop friendships outside your own ministry.

Be away on Sunday.
Pass up an opportunity to worry.
Take a walk for fun rather than exercise.
Study the Word except to teach it.
Spend an evening at home alone.

BELIEVE
All you hear about the former pastor's wife.
That people will never move away.
That nursery workers will never forget.
That people will schedule vacations around the church calendar.
That you must have special music at every service.
That you can keep your house deacon-ready all the time.
That you are always right.
That you are always wrong.
That you can make others do right.
That when they do wrong, it's your fault.

FORGET
To laugh. To cry.
To play. To pray.
That the devil is a mean old booger, and a liar besides.
That your Father loves you.
That He has everything under control.
That people are human.
That you are, too.
That attendance at the Looney Reunion is optional.

26
Home

The emergency room was busy, so my wait had been long. Finally I was called to the desk to answer a long string of questions before I could see a doctor. As we moved down the list, the young man helping me began to look more and more bewildered.

He stopped, looked up, and said, "Mrs. Barba, you have an Indiana address, a South Carolina phone number, a Tennessee driver's license, and you're at a North Carolina hospital." And he stared at me, expecting some sort of explanation. But I was feeling awfully sick and it was all terribly complicated, so I just responded, "Does that seem strange to you? It does to me, too." And I left it at that.

I have had similar experiences when meeting strangers who ask politely and innocently, "Where are you from?" It's a simple question, but the answer requires a paragraph and more details than they want to hear, for every few months, my husband and I move our RV to a city where a new church is being planted and make that town our temporary home. Many cities are now familiar to me, but I really belong to none of them. I have no hometown.

So I have often wondered—do I live everywhere or nowhere? Am I always at home or never at home? After thinking it through, I have arrived at a comforting conclusion: I am always at home, for home isn't a place at all. It's a Person!

Home is a place to live . . . I dwell in Him (Psalm 90:1).
Home is where families gather . . . He is my Father and I am
  His child (1 John 3:2).
Home is safety . . . He is my refuge (Psalm 91:9).
Home is tranquility . . . He is my peace (Ephesians 2:14).
Home is belonging . . . I am "accepted in the beloved"
  (Ephesians 1:6).
Home is security . . . I am a "sheep of His pasture"
  (Psalm 100:3).

Maybe you're called to serve the Lord in a familiar, hometown setting. More often, though, He leads His servants away from the comfortable and customary to a place where the scenery is strange, the accents alien, and the customs peculiar. If that's your assignment, do you ever yearn for home? Take heart—home is closer than you think.

> From here to there, and then from there to here
> The people of this planet circling roam,
> And I as well—but oh, one truth is clear:
> I live in God, and God Himself is Home.
>
> From hither and from thither comes the call,
> Perhaps to places near, perhaps abroad,
> But anywhere I am, and through it all
> My heart's at home, for Home is Sovereign God.
>   —Anne Ortlund

27
Errors

"Take me out to the ballgame; take me out with the crowd! Buy me some peanuts and . . ."

Actually, I'll go even if you won't buy me peanuts, because I really do like watching baseball, especially small town, minor league games. At my kind of baseball game, the stadium seats are painted red, white, and blue and the moon rises over the right field fence. Front row seats are cheap; hot dogs cost a dollar. When somebody hits a home run, we drop dollar bills in a hat as a bonus to his meager salary.

Minor league games are fun because they are unpredictable, and they are unpredictable because young ballplayers make lots of errors. Base runners slide frantically into home but miss the plate. Pitchers pitch at a blazing 90 mph—way over the catcher's head. Infielders snag a groundball and fire away to the wrong base. Outfielders take their eyes off a soaring fly ball, and it drops at their feet. One after another, errors happen, and each is tallied on the scoreboard under a large "E."

Some fans jeer errors, but not me. I cringe in sympathy, because I, too, am dreadfully error-prone. I drop the ball by forgetting my duties or doing them poorly. I do the right thing at the wrong time. I blurt out tactless, thoughtless words. I fall on my embarrassed face over and over, and of course, the bigger my audience, the bigger my gaffe. Blunders, slip-ups, boo-boos — no matter what you call them, they are all humiliating. I'm just glad that my errors aren't tallied for public amusement and you are too polite to heckle.

My lame-brained moments seem worse because I'm a ministry wife. I'm supposed to be a good example, after all, and people do seem to expect more of me than of an ordinary mortal. I try my best to be perfect, so why do I keep goofing up? Paul echoes my frustration in Romans 7: "For the good that I will to do, I do not do; but the evil I will not to do, that I practice . . . .Oh, wretched [wo]man that I am!"

Why does the Lord let me continue to act like a doofus? It's because He has something better in mind for me: conformity to His image. He doesn't expect perfection from sadly-human me. But because He loves me too much to leave me just as I am, He is continually refining and sanctifying me. Through my blunders, He shows me my deficiencies so I'll be eager for His filling. Mistakes will speed my growth if I will handle them in a godly way.

After an error, I first need to talk to the Lord Who promises pardon, and then to the others my failure has hurt. I have watched erring baseball players at the end of an inning mumble apologies to teammates as they trot back to the dugout. In the ministry, too, there's no substitute for prompt, candid admission of fault, and no greater relief than forgiveness.

Then I need to ignore the urge to quit the team. After all, everybody will goof up now and then. "In many things we all offend" (James 3:2). After I fall, I ought to just get up and press on. No matter how humiliated I feel, I "shall not be utterly cast down, for the Lord upholdeth [me] with His hand" (Psalm 37:24).

And then I should quickly shake it off. If I wallow in self-condemnation, I'll be too distracted to prepare for the next pitch. The best player, on the field or in the ministry, resolutely forgets what's behind (but not its lesson) and reaches toward what's ahead (becoming like Christ).

Until I'm in heaven with Him, like Him, I'll be just a minor league player, doing my best but appallingly fallible. Be patient with me, and I'll do the same for you. We are, after all, on the same team.

28
Comfort

"I've been where you are, and I know how you feel."

Those words are sweet to the ears of a woman in pain. When she hears them, the sorrow squeezing her heart eases a bit. Someone has been through this, and since that someone is alive and talking, there must be life after pain. The hope is born that maybe she too will survive.

Anyone who sincerely says those words is automatically in ministry—for to minister means to serve, to aid, to help, to comfort, to care for with gentle understanding. One who has ached knows best how to soothe another's painful throbbing. One who has stumbled knows how to gently lift one who's also down. One who has cried knows how to wipe tears.

When a hurting woman hears those words, she realizes that she won't be criticized when she expresses her anguish. She's free to be candid, to say without fear how she's really feeling. She won't be scolded for crying or rebuked for grieving. Her comforter has been there and knows what it's like.

"I've been where you are, and I know how you feel."

They are wonderful words, with astonishing power to mend a broken heart. And you, my friend, are usually the one given the privilege of saying them, as the God of all comfort allows you to use your painful experiences as tools to comfort others (2 Corinthians 1:3-4). But when you're the one who is hurting, who comforts you?

If your pain is related to your ministry, there may be no other female within hugging distance who can honestly say she has been where you are, for the pitfalls and problems unique to our calling can be fully understood only by someone who's also been in the ministry. If you have a godly mentor you can call on and cry with, shout hooray! She's a priceless gift. Cherish her. Share her with the rest of us!

If you don't—and even if you do—remember this: no matter what you are going through, Jesus knows how you feel. He has been in ministry on this earth and He knows what it's like. He worked with sinners (and still does). Most didn't follow Him (and still don't). They were often ungrateful and unresponsive. They disappointed Him and rejected His love. Nothing you face in ministry is unfamiliar to Him.

So when you hurt, come to His throne and pour out your heart. Be transparent. He will listen without condemning and comfort without censuring. He is your compassionate and faithful High Priest, and His ears are open to your cry (Psalm 34:15).

Then sit still in the silence of your pain and know that He is God. Wait expectantly for His tender words of comfort. They'll come, and they'll probably be something like this: *"I've been where you are, and I know how you feel."*

29
Tattoos

What's so special about Rosie? I have no idea—but that huge man loved her enough to have her name tattooed in ornate crimson letters on his bulky bicep. Nobody has ever loved me that much. Or (more likely) the people who love me are just not the tattooing type.

Tattoos are appearing more often these days. I've casually and unobtrusively (I hope) taken notice of them in unexpected places on unlikely people—a miniature purple elephant squatting on the ankle of a young mom; a scaly, fire-breathing dragon perched on the arm of an otherwise ordinary-looking grandma; and a fearsome snake coiled around the leg of a middle-aged hairdresser. I've gawked at other more mysterious and bizarre designs engraved on skin.

I am not interested in becoming a tattooed lady, but I am fascinated. What motivates this strange urge? Is that hairdresser sure she'll always find her resident rattlesnake stunning? Is Grandma convinced her dragon makes her look younger? Does the young mom still collect purple elephants? And does that big guy still love Rosie?

I hope so, because a tattoo is a lifetime commitment—cheap to get but expensive, risky, and maybe even impossible to remove. Other keepsakes of failed romances and passing interests can be tossed, but not a tattoo. It's permanent. It may turn into an unrelenting reminder of a person or occasion you'd rather forget. Minds and values change, but tattoos remain.

I'm weary of being encircled by body-billboards, so weary that I've been tempted to point out their ugliness to tattooed strangers. So to keep from embarrassing myself, I have made a decision. I will let others' tattoos be a reminder to me of Isaiah 49:16: "Behold, I have graven thee upon the palms of My hands." Just as some Jews had an emblem of their beloved Jerusalem permanently imprinted on their hands, the Lord says to His beloved ones, "You are written on My palms."

What does He see on His palms? My name—my face? Whatever it is, it's a symbol of His love. I am His; He is mine. On His hands, painfully inscribed by the piercing nails of the cross, is an emblem of His eternal commitment and devotion to me, a mark of our inseparable union.

It's an insignia of His steadfast promises. With those gentle hands, He leads me and holds me (Psalm 139:10). His almighty hands are my security (John 10:28-29). The strong right hand of His righteousness keeps me on my feet (Isaiah 41:10) and has unlimited power to work on my behalf (Isaiah 59:1). His commitment to me is more than lifelong; it is eternal.

What's so special about me? Not a thing, except that the God of the universe loves me and delights in taking care of me! That says nothing at all about me, but everything about Him. When all earthly tattoos and what they represent are faded and forgotten, He, through the exceeding riches of His grace, will still remember me.

30
What Did You Do All Day?

"So what did you do all day?"

What? What? What did I do all day? I knew the question was simply a way of opening dinner conversation and that my family wasn't checking to see that I earned my room and board, but the question still annoyed me. My exhausted self wanted to holler in answer, "Look around and see!"

I'm glad I held off on the hollering, for except for supper—and it was rapidly disappearing—they could not have seen anything I had done all day. All the tasks that had consumed my time and energy were invisible.

I transformed laundry from dirty jumbles hidden in hampers into clean stacks hidden in drawers. My rag and I banished household dust. (Where did it go?) My vacuum and I evicted under-bed dust bunnies. I carted trash to the curb, and it disappeared down the street in a truck.

I reorganized an unnoticed closet shelf and removed obscure stains from the edges of sofa cushions. I shopped for a cartful of groceries, brought them home, and hid them away in the pantry, fridge, and freezer. I mended an inside pocket of my husband's dress slacks and fed the houseplants with invisible fertilizer. I unclogged a sluggish pipe, and the gunk had rapidly vanished down the drain. Even the wrinkles I had ironed out had disappeared. And who would notice that all the beds now had clean sheets?

I answered the mail, but there was no neat stack of stamped and sealed envelopes to prove my diligence, since the letters had traveled through cyber-space. Plans I had made for a Bible study and luncheon were rattling around in my brain, not on paper. I proofread Sunday school lessons hidden in computer files and bought virtual airline e-tickets for my husband's preaching trip. No one had heard me practice an offertory or review my scripture verses. And nobody overheard the counseling, encouraging, and checking-up done in telephone calls sandwiched between my other tasks.

All I had done that day were the unseen chores of any ministry wife, the private ones that greatly outnumber her visible duties. Though each was mundane on its own, together they added up to a day well spent. Maybe they were even more significant for being humanly invisible, for those who serve "with eyeservice, as menpleasers" don't receive the reward that comes from serving the Lord Christ (Colossians 3:22-24). And the God of the universe did see them. He is not so unjust that He will forget to honor all loving ministry, no matter how commonplace, done for His children (Hebrews 6:10).

I didn't detail my long list of accomplishments to my family. They were too busy making their supper disappear. Maybe tomorrow I'll can some tomatoes or crochet something or just post my scratched-off to-do list. But even if they never notice, it's enough for me to know that the Master is watching, and that He knows what I've been up to all day.

31
Typing

My computer is my friend—a helpful comrade and compliant servant. I appreciate all it does for me, but two of its little keys, I adore! To understand why, you had to have learned to type the way I did, on a manual typewriter in a 1960s high school typing class.

Typing I found easy, but typing flawlessly I found impossible. Since we were expected to turn in papers with no visible corrections, erasing was a skill I learned early and used often. My stiff rubber eraser was a flat disk, with a brush attached to sweep away eraser crumbs and paper dust. I would type and re-type, type and re-type, erase and erase and erase until there were holes in my paper and in my good humor.

Those clackety, cumbersome machines lacked the miraculous *backspace* and *delete* keys found on my laptop. They did have a key labeled *backspace,* but all it could do was laboriously reverse the carriage one space at a time. Finding and fixing mistakes was up to me and my awkward eraser. And as for *delete*—well, that was only a futuristic fantasy.

When correctible typing paper was invented that needed only a pencil eraser, it seemed like a gift from heaven. Soon correction fluid, correction tape, and (wow! amazing!) self-correcting electric typewriters came along to save time and my sanctification. But none of those innovations compare to my beloved *backspace* and *delete*. Now when I misspell a word, my helpful computer discreetly underlines it. I press one key, and presto — the goof is gone! When I find errors on my own, it's incredibly easy to delete them and begin again.

I'm considering having two keys installed on my ministry-wife forehead. Then at the end of every day, I can simply backspace to my poor decisions, hasty words, and wasted opportunities and try again. Or I could backspace even further to the most dismal moments of my past and discover how God's providence was even then working all things together for my good.

A mental *delete* key would be useful, too. I could erase everyday ministry discouragements and record instead, in bold italics, all His blessings. I could erase memories of self-inflicted failures but save those of faith-empowered successes. When the devil reminds me of confessed and forsaken sins, I could just press *delete* and do as God does: remember them no more. After all, those sins have been eternally erased, without even any eraser crumbs or paper dust left behind as evidence.

Maybe it wasn't such a bad way to learn typing after all. I didn't gain just keyboard skills; I learned patience through tribulation! And even more than others, I appreciate the marvels of computerized word-processing. I will never take for granted the wonders of *backspace* and *delete*, on the keyboard and in my walk with God.

32
Blueprints

She stands on the building site of her life, blueprints in hand. She has been drawing them since she first held a crayon, and though they have been modified and refined over the years, they now are complete and highly detailed.

She rarely has to refer to them anymore, since they are engraved in her mind. She knows more or less which perfect, handsome man she will marry and what sort of job he will have, with sufficient income, of course, to pay for the house she has already designed. She has planned how many attractive children she will have and at what intervals. They will be healthy, intelligent, talented, obedient children with flawless manners. She even knows their names.

She was surprised when her husband turned out to be in the ministry, but she soon incorporated that change into her blueprints. Their ministry, she decided, would be a model for others. The congregation would love and follow their shepherd. She would be an ideal ministry wife, and at home, a modern Proverbs 31 woman. The entire community would rise and call her blessed. It was all right there in her blueprints.

But then the oddest thing happened. Building materials she hadn't ordered appeared on her life's construction site and the Master Builder began to erect a building around her that didn't resemble her meticulous plans — not one little bit.

The house He built for her is nothing like the dream house she envisioned and nowhere near the lot she had staked out. Despite her best efforts, it is often untidy. Its inhabitants have turned out to be defective (including herself, to her surprise). Some of the sheep are wandering and blaming it on the shepherd. People call her all the time, but few call her blessed.

At first she was simply startled, certain that if she drew God's attention to His errors, He'd correct them. She held up her blueprints: "Ummmm . . . I'm afraid you have made a few mistakes. See, right here on my plan. . ." But the Builder just smiled gently and continued building according to His own flawless, higher thoughts and ways, constructing a life that didn't conform to her plans at all.

Bewildered and frustrated, she now has a choice to make. She can live a joyless martyr's life in her unwelcome abode, grimly accepting her dismal fate, silently indulging her self-pity. Or she can plop down and pout, sticking out her lip, and complain bitterly to anyone who will listen — including the Builder. Or she can shake her fist at Him and stomp off in fury to construct her own life according to her own blueprints. (And He may allow her to go, but then send leanness to her soul.)

There's one more possibility, of course, and that's what she decides to do. After one last, longing look at her beloved blueprints, she tears them up. As the scraps of paper blow away, so does her unhappiness. She turns and walks contentedly into the house that God built. And there she lives, happily ever after.

33
Did You See the Preacher's Wife?

She's the lady who, though she knows all the words to all the verses of all the hymns, still holds the hymnbook open during the congregational singing—as a good example.

She's the lady who lugged a load of paraphernalia to church but forgot her Bible so grabbed one from a shelf in her husband's office without noticing it was in Hebrew. She still looked at the unintelligible sermon text when she was supposed to—as a good example. She silenced her children with a look when this sent them into a giggle fit.

She's the lady who wore to church a new dress found on clearance, which she was careful to explain to anyone who noticed. And everyone did, because she's the preacher's wife. (She bought two others at the same time but will widely space their debuts.)

She's the lady who made clandestine signals to the preacher that his microphone was turned off, his tie was askew, and a fly had landed on his forehead. Only he recognized her signals, but the rest of the congregation was noticeably relieved.

She's the lady who shook hands at the church door beside her preacher husband, slipping him a breath mint as folks approached and antibacterial hand gel when they'd gone. At her post she collected others' heart burdens to carry but kept her own a Lord-shared secret. She smiled and smiled and smiled, especially at those who didn't deserve it.

She's the lady who even in her new dresses would never think she looks like a model, but actually is one—a Romans 12 model of tender affection and habitual deference, of energetic and warm-hearted service, of hope and patience in trials, of persistence in prayer. She is known for looking for needs she can meet and ways to show loving hospitality, for crying when others cry and laughing when they laugh, for seeking out the lonely and lowly to make them her friends. She is not conceited. In fact, she wonders why anyone would think she is special.

But she is. In fact, she's extraordinary. Next time you see her, would you tell her that for me?

34
Mary

You see her in manger scenes everywhere during the Christmas season—Mary, lit by a bulb glowing somewhere inside her translucent plastic self. She wears a blue robe. She has serenely folded hands and a halo glowing above her veiled head. She smiles benevolently at her cherubic child. When I see her planted on lawns and mantles, I wonder— was Mary as tranquil as she looks?

When she appeared on the streets of Nazareth great with child, the hometown gossips got busy. Did the whispered doubts of others with their intimation that she was deluded lead to uncertainties of her own? Did this very young woman ever stare into the night sky and see question marks in the stars, wondering if maybe she had seen Gabriel and heard his announcement only in her imagination?

At the end of an exhausting late-pregnancy trek to a strange city teeming with travelers, handling her labor pains alone while Joseph begged for a room—any room—where she could deliver, did she inwardly moan, "What am I doing here? I want to go home. I want my mother!"

Laying her newborn in the straw of a feeding trough, was she disappointed that it was not a cradle crafted by her carpenter husband? When frantic, heavy-breathing shepherds rushed in, crowding close to touch the angel-announced newborn, did she long for a clean, private place to nurse her son?

Perhaps she drew a relieved breath as she entered the temple with Joseph to make a dedication offering for 40-day old Jesus. Finally, something normal, this familiar custom of Jewish law. But then a strange old man startled her by taking the baby Jesus from her arms and prophesying over Him in a loud voice, ending with a warning to Mary that heart-piercing anguish was in her future.

Was anguish what she felt when, from the safety of exile in Egypt, she learned of Herod's slaughter of Bethlehem infants? Did her heart break for the mothers whose children were being murdered because of Herod's jealous rage toward her own little boy? Think of her pain as she saw Jesus rejected by her other children. And what happened in her heart when she discovered that her own religious authorities were plotting His murder? Contemplate the courage it took to follow the mob to Calvary and of her agony as she wept at the cross of her tortured, innocent firstborn.

Artists depict her as a delicate creature in a flowing gown, but it would be more realistic to dress her in sturdy denim, for this woman had a backbone of steel. Life wasn't easy for Mary. So was she miserable, frustrated by events out of her control and contrary to her plans? Was she enraged by the injustice of it all? I don't think so. After all, a bondslave doesn't expect an easy life, and that's what she called herself in Luke 1:38 — "the handmaid of the Lord."

She had feelings, of course, like any female. And I suspect that this woman of contemplative disposition, who knew how to treasure up thoughts for private reflection (Luke

2:19), may have had an even deeper emotional well than most of us. But when she surrendered her will to Jehovah, she also surrendered her feelings and then simply obeyed.

Was it worth it? Someday we can ask her. Mary, the only human present with Jesus at both His birth and His death, has now been with Him in glory for over 20 centuries. We will meet her there. I don't know how the mother of the Messiah is honored in heaven, but even on earth, even among those who do not love her Son, she is revered as the ideal of motherhood.

So the next time you spot a Mary modeled of plastic, ceramic, crystal, or paper, take a moment to think about the flesh and blood Mary, a model sacrificial servant of the Savior. How I thank Him for Mary, and for you, her sister handmaid of the Lord.

35
Slapout

Have you ever been to Slapout? That Alabama crossroads was our temporary home while we helped a nearby church planter. Slapout has friendly people, a pretty lake, and a funny name. It was named, they say, for a local store too small to carry a full line of provisions. When asked for an uncommon item, rather than admitting he didn't carry it, the shopkeeper would claim it was out of stock. "Sorry," he'd say, "I'm slap out."

I don't know much about shopkeeping, but *slap out* is a notion I do understand, for that's how I feel when facing extra-heavy ministry demands--slap out of the resources I need to do my job.

During those times, I'm convinced I can't handle one more trial. If I sense a new heartache approaching, I want to say, "Go away! I'm slap out of endurance, and I have no patience for you." Or I spy the devil arriving with a fresh army of temptations, and still wounded from our last skirmish, I want to surrender. "I can't fight you anymore, you old devil. I'm slap out of courage."

There are days when I'm convinced I can't make even one more decision, for there's not a smidgen of wisdom left in my stash. When yet another needy person arrives for help, I discover I've already doled out so much compassion to others that my stock of sympathy is depleted. I spot heavy ministry demands heading my way (grumblers to pacify, conflicts to resolve, programs to plan, lessons to study, company to entertain), and I'm tempted to slam the door on all of them. "Sorry, can't help you. I'm slap out!"

Of course I am. Such emptiness only proves that "in me (that is, in my flesh) nothing good dwells" (Romans 7:18). Pride tells me I'm sufficient in myself, but pride is a liar. What I am tempted to call my competence for ministry is actually only "His strength made perfect in my weakness" (2 Corinthians 12:9). In my own strength, I'm like a shop with vacant shelves, unable to supply myself, much less have anything to share with others.

That's the truth, and there's no shame in admitting it. After all, I'm not meant to be the source; I'm simply a channel. God is the Source—the willing and unfailing Supplier of all good gifts for service. I just have to stop fretting long enough to remember that. When I acknowledge that all the springs of my faith, all my capacity for ministry and good works, are in Him (Psalm 87:7), He fills my heart from His infinite store of riches in glory until my cup runs over. Then, restocked and replenished, I'm once again ready and eager to serve all my customers.

I come for help in humility and yet with boldness, for He has given me His unfailing promise to supply all I need to do His will. And He, unlike the rest of us, is never slap out!

36
A Broken Heart

What good is a broken heart? That's what I asked myself as I looked down at what was supposed to be a special Valentine's Day dessert—a rich chocolate cake, so gooey and sweet that it needed no frosting.

I thought I had carefully followed the recipe. I blended the batter and poured it into my heart-shaped baking pan. But I must not have done the "grease and flour pan" part well enough. Cooling on the counter after baking, the cake looked flawless, but when I turned it out onto a plate, it broke in half, with a jagged, crooked, crumbly crack right down the middle.

Well, I thought, I have broken my own heart. That's a new one. Usually, other people do it for me. Now what do I do? What good is a broken heart?

Actually, a broken heart is priceless. It guarantees special intimacy with the Lord, for He has promised to be "near to those who have a broken heart." He hears the cry of a crushed spirit and comes close to relieve its pain.

A ministry wife with a broken heart will find it a useful tool, filled with soothing balm received from the God of all comfort—balm she can dispense to help heal others' wounds.

And a broken heart makes an excellent gift for the Lord. Old Testament worshippers brought Him burnt offerings chosen from the wheat, oil, salt, and animals He had provided for them "day by day without fail." These were good gifts, given back to the Lord with a thankful heart.

But sometimes His gifts seem more like calamities. When He allows painful circumstances to arrive "day by day without fail," our hearts and spirits break. If we can find a way to offer our brokenness back to Him with submission and thanksgiving, we can transform our pain into a sweet sacrifice, a more acceptable offering than bulls and goats could ever be. "For You do not desire sacrifice . . . You do not delight in burnt offering. The sacrifices of God are a broken spirit, a broken and a contrite heart—these, O God, You will not despise."

What did I do with my broken heart? I mixed up a bowl of sticky frosting and used it like glue to re-attach the jagged pieces. After I had smeared the whole cake with frosting, nobody could tell I had botched the Valentine dessert. They did notice that it was extra-sweet, though, and that's the way it goes with broken hearts, for when the Lord "heals the brokenhearted, and binds up their wounds," He adds a sweetness that can come no other way.

Now that I know how to repair a broken cake, I'm not afraid to try that recipe again. And remembering what God can do, I'm no longer afraid of trouble, for I know that a broken heart can be a very good thing.

(2 Corinthians 1:3-4, Psalm 34:17-19, Psalm 51:16-17, Psalm 147:3)

37
Loneliness

Those "saints of old" — were they ever lonely?

Obediently hammering and sawing away for 128 years, while almost everyone on earth thought he was a lunatic, was Noah lonely?

When Abraham left home and family for the absolutely unknown just because God told him to, did he suffer the ache of loneliness? Leaving his servants behind, trudging toward the place of sacrifice with his son and heir of promise — knife in hand — did he feel alone?

And Hagar, weeping bitterly in the wilderness of Beersheba as her child lay dying under a shrub — did she think she too would soon die alone in that wasteland?

Consider Moses' isolation on the backside of the desert. He knew his exile was due to his own failure but didn't know those years would end at 40. Did he believe himself permanently separated from his own people?

Job knew not only the loneliness of sorrow and disease, but also a painful distance from God caused by complete bewilderment at His working. Harassed by his wife, mocked by his enemies, blamed by his friends, Job grieved alone.

Running from furious Queen Jezebel, cowering under a juniper tree in exhaustion and depression, Elijah expressed desperate loneliness when he moaned: "I, even I only, remain."

Was Daniel lonely in the lion's den? Jeremiah, in the muddy pit? Or Paul, three years alone in Arabia? And how about our Savior? Hanging on the cross, abandoned by His friends and forsaken by His Father, Jesus endured the loneliest hours in history.

Are you ever lonely? Loneliness follows even the most dedicated ministry wife through church doors and to the mission field, into offices and schoolrooms, to showers, weddings, and retreats. In the grocery store and in the pew, she senses the apartness of being a spiritual leader. Loneliness is common to her calling.

But since God created her to crave and enjoy companionship, how can she endure loneliness? She can seek God! Even the loneliest woman who seeks Him hungrily will soon be satisfied, for He will come to fulfill all her longings. She who seeks Him silently will hear His voice. She who searches for Him early will find her thirst for companionship quenched by the sweet water of His presence.

To lonely saints in scripture, He came! He came with a validating flood and a covenant promise. He supplied a lamb and a well of water. He spoke from a burning bush and a whirlwind. He brought food and drink, reassurance and resurrection. At their moments of greatest loneliness, He came as Deliverer, Promise-Keeper, and Friend, showing Himself true and proving Himself enough.

And this God is your God. If He is allowing you to be lonely right now, maybe it's because He craves your company. Seek Him, and soon your heart will be singing, "Whom have I in heaven but Thee? And there is none upon earth that I desire beside Thee. My flesh and my heart faileth, but God is the strength of my heart, and my portion forever" (Psalm 73:25-26).

38
A Dry Stick

She's the perfect ministry wife: bursting with love, constantly sacrificing her desires, time, and energy for others. She's full of joy, ceaselessly in a state of quiet delight. No matter what happens in her home or ministry, her heart knows only perfect peace. Her patience has no limit, even when tried by awful aggravations and annoyances.

She's unfailingly kind and compassionate even to the most irritating people and has impeccable manners. You can count on her; she never lets anyone down or neglects a task. Her emotions (as well as her tongue and appetite) are under control. And yet she doesn't know how fine a person she is. She's so unassuming that she'd be genuinely surprised to hear herself called "humble."

I'd like to be that lady. Maybe you are. But I'm not. I'm flawed and fallible instead. I do try to love people, and most of the time, I do. But people can be demanding, and I crave time and space to do as I please. As for "ceaseless delight" and "perfect peace" — well, occasional calmness and intermittent tranquility more accurately describe my state of mind.

Though I'm not deliberately rude, I do sometimes forget my manners and show impatience with infuriating people. I also occasionally forget duties (only important ones, of course). I'm embarrassed to admit it, but my self-discipline regularly fails when confronted by chocolate, a chance to gossip, or any opportunity to feel sorry for myself. And I enjoy praise, especially for my humility.

Wretched me. What can I do? I know that despair is not the answer, and I'd rather not be a quitter. But I get frustrated, for though I long to be an abundant fruit-bearer, I often find myself a dry stick instead.

A dry stick is just a branch that stopped hanging on. That's a branch's only job, you see: to stay connected so that the life of the vine can flow through it. Without that crucial connection, it withers into a useless stick, for a disconnected branch "cannot bear fruit of itself" (John 15:4).

When a branch hangs on, though, amazing things happen. Fruit appears at unexpected times and places. When the branch would normally be irritated, she is loving instead. She's surprised by the arrival of joy when she'd ordinarily be grumpy and by peace when she expects anxiety. And patience, gentleness, goodness, faithfulness, meekness, self-control—all that lovely fruit of the Spirit ripens at just the right moment. Nobody is more surprised than the branch, but everyone is blessed.

I have learned that I can't produce my own fruit, but if all I have to do is hang on, I can manage that. I can stick my nose in the Book and stay there a while. I can pray without ceasing. I can meditate on God rather than pondering my problems. I can abide in—stay close to—hang onto—the Vine. I may never become the perfect ministry wife, but that's okay. I know I'll be more pleasant to live with and more pleasing to the Vinedresser as a fruitful branch than as an old dry stick.

39
Listening to a Liar

I sat in a pew listening to the piano prelude, suffering from the glooms. Our church plant had been a source of heavy trials. Some were of the typical new-church variety, but others were completely and bewilderingly new. We were under satanic assault, and sadly, I was more victim than victor.

Down my aisle tottered a friend, a ministry widow who had often been my helper and encourager. She stopped for a quick hug, looked into my eyes, and asked how I was doing. I decided to be completely candid. "I'm miserable. The devil is attacking from every direction, and I don't know what to do."

"What to do? What to do? You don't know what to do?" Her gentle face changed into that of a warrior and her voice rose as she stood taller, held her cane like a spear, and raised her big black Bible. "You take up your sword of the Spirit and your shield of faith, and you ADVANCE! That's what you do!"

Then she stopped abruptly, lowered her props, smiled sweetly, and went on down the aisle, leaving me surprised, amused, and suddenly so energized and encouraged that I wanted to laugh out loud.

Of course! How could I have forgotten? The devil is no match for the One Who lives in me! I had been listening to inward whispers of looming failure and defeat, believing them true. But they were lies instead—the deceits of the father of all falsehood, the master of masquerade. He's a nasty, cruel enemy, but even Satan with all his wiles is no equal to one woman armed with truth and faith in the power of its Author. How foolish I had been to listen to lies and live in defeat.

Have you been hearing Satan's lies, too? Most ministry wives do. What is he saying? Are they disheartening words about yourself, your family, your ministry? No matter how intense Satan's assault, nothing can separate you from the One Who loves you, and through Him, you are more than a conqueror! Choose promises of God to use as ammunition and keep them close at hand. When you detect lies creeping into your brain, take up your sword and shield and ADVANCE!

It was easy to see that my friend was experienced at what she demonstrated. She'd had plenty of practice, for as long as she had been a ministry wife, she had been a prime target of a dangerously real adversary who's been at this since Eden. You are Satan's target, too, for he knows that if he can make you his victim, he will have infiltrated the home of one of God's front-line soldiers. Your defeated spirit will spread through your family and into your ministry, and the enemy's plot will have succeeded.

But he doesn't have to win. If a sweet little old lady with a big black Bible can be a strong and contagious conqueror, so can you, for your confidence is never in your own might, or your own courage, but in an almighty God Who is always at work for you, and Who, unlike the enemy, always tells the truth.

40
Doing Too Much

You might be doing too much if . . .

You have never seen the bottom of your laundry hamper. You suspect it doesn't have one.

Clothes that have to be ironed are always worn warm.

By the time you sew on the button, your child has outgrown the shirt.

Your mother asks, "Who is this?" when you call.

You once gave a belated birthday card to your husband.

All your cookbooks feature 15-minute meals.

When you finally sit down at the dinner table, you reach to fasten your seat belt.

The berries you bought for making jam died of terminal mold instead.

Some days, Excedrin and coffee are your bread and water.

A 20-minute traffic delay shatters your day's schedule.

You enjoy church partly because it's a chance to sit.

You have been known to arrive at church in your slippers.

You scribble your grocery list on the bulletin during the offering.

Coupons expire while crumpled in your purse.

You have wrapped a gift while driving to the baby shower.

You wish your brain had an on/off switch.

You'd never wake up without an alarm.

Sickness just means running a little more slowly.

You return exhausted from vacation.

No matter what you are doing, you feel that you should be doing something else.

If you're doing too much . . .

You'll quickly lose the joys of ministry done "heartily, as to the Lord."

His Spirit's sweet fruit will sour in your frantic heart.

Your health will suffer. (A chicken running around with its head cut off is headed for KFC.)

You'll be too busy doing what's urgent to do what's needful.

You'll stop doing too much when . . .

You slam the door on the thief of hurry.

You stop hearing every human request as a divine command.

You keep your priority list posted right side up.

You master the gentle art of asking for help.

You discover that exhaustion is rarely the route to success.

You stop believing it all depends on you.

You follow the Master from your frazzled race to His desert place and there ask Him to teach you to do just exactly enough.

41
Sweetness

"You're so *sweet!*"

The lady who said this to me meant it as a compliment, but in those early days of ministry, I wasn't flattered. Sweet meant syrupy and maudlin. Slushy, mushy, squishy. I'd rather have been called capable, competent, or clever.

I am wiser now. I long to be sweet, because I have learned that to be genuinely sweet is to be like the One Who gave Himself "an offering and a sacrifice to God for a sweet-smelling savor" (Ephesians 5:2).

Such sweetness comes only through sacrifice and brokenness. The sweet fragrance of the cross, after all, rose from a place of death. When I take up my own cross to follow Him, I can expect to die. But I don't die eagerly or easily, and I expect you don't, either. The only way for either of us to become sweet is to let God do it.

First I must present myself to Him as a living sacrifice. That's no great gift, for "in me (that is, in my flesh) dwells no good thing" (Romans 7:18). In my natural state, I'm more like one of those weird substances that perfume-makers collect as bases for expensive scents — odious, disgusting raw materials like ambergris (I'll spare you the wretched details).

He accepts me, though, stinky as I am, and goes to work making me sweet.

The sweetening process then involves brokenness. In a perfumer's lab, herbs, flowers, resins, spices, and aromatic oils are cut, chopped, ground, shredded, crushed, heated, boiled, separated, evaporated, clarified, and concentrated. Those beaten and broken ingredients are proportioned carefully and blended skillfully into the base until the final product conforms to the master perfumer's ideal of perfume perfection.

And so the loving Master stirs into my days a precise medley of difficulties, sorrows, disappointments, and heartbreaks, adding them gently and in right measure until I am conformed to the image of our sweet Savior, Who was "stricken, smitten of God and afflicted . . . wounded for our transgressions . . . bruised for our iniquities" (Isaiah 53:4-5).

Only God can make me sweet, but if I let Him, He will — not so others will praise me, but so believers and unbelievers alike will detect in me the sweet scent of Christ. As I diffuse His fragrance in every place, He'll get the glory, not me. And when somebody tells me I'm sweet, I still won't be flattered. I'll be surprised. And grateful.

42
Sunday Picnic

"Mommy, I wish we wasn't Christians."

The words coming from my sweet little girl in the back seat surprised me. I turned and followed her gaze out the car window toward the neighbors' house, and then I understood. It was still quite early on Sunday morning, but we were already on our way to church. Our neighbors were still asleep, but their daughter had told Stephanie all about their exciting plans for an all-day Sunday picnic at the lake.

We were heading into a busy day of multiple services, rehearsals, and meetings, which for my daughter would mean long hours of sitting, listening, and waiting for grownups. I'm not sure what I said to lift her spirits as we drove to church. Platitudes, probably, and reminders of the fun of Sunday school, of seeing her friends and singing in the children's choir. I do remember a sigh in my own spirit, though. On that sunny morning, a picnic at the lake sounded mighty good to me, too.

I knew Sunday would be long and exhausting, and if things went as usual, spiritually draining as well. At church I would see not only the people I loved for their steady faithfulness and constant encouragement, but I'd also see people I loved who weren't doing right, and my burden for them would leave me with my usual Sunday heartache. And I'd battle with my frustration toward those I'd see only in my mind: the indifferent or unreliable ones who could have been at church but weren't.

The realities of ministering to very human beings can cause any of us to think now and then, "I wish we wasn't in ministry." Whenever that happens to me, recalling some old, old stories keeps me from quitting.

Leading Israel through the wilderness was no picnic for Moses. The continual murmuring, quarreling, fretting, and fault-finding caused him to moan to Jehovah, "I am not able to bear all these people. The burden is too heavy for me. Just go ahead and let me die!" (Numbers 11:14-15).

David, distressed by spiteful enemies and false friends, wished for "wings like a dove. . . [to] fly away and be at rest . . . wander far off, and remain in the wilderness" (Psalm 55:6-7).

Jeremiah had wept over Israel until he had no more tears. But their callous unresponsiveness caused even this compassionate prophet to yearn to operate "a lodging place for travelers" in the wilderness, "that I might leave my people and go from them" (Jeremiah 9:2). I have felt like that a time or two.

I can also identify with Paul's "desire to depart and be with Christ, which is far better." But Paul, like those other ministry heroes, decided to do what was "more needful": stay, pray, work, and trust (Philippians 1:23-24). He didn't quit, understanding that though the ministry is no picnic, it is most certainly worthwhile. And seeing lives change because you've let the Lord use you is much more fun than any picnic could ever be!

Some days in the ministry, the only good thing that happens is that you don't quit. I hope that for you, those days are few. But when they come, and you've just about decided to run away to the lake, resolutely point your car toward church instead. As you drive, listen carefully, and you may hear the sound of a great cloud of witnesses. It's those old heroes of the faith, cheering you on.

43
Two Broken Thermometers

The digital thermometer on our car's dashboard is broken. Poor little thing hasn't been the same since that day in the desert when it accurately read 116 degrees. Now it soars and drops at will.

It doesn't bother me anymore. It's just one minor defect in an otherwise reliable car, and in fact it's become a mild source of entertainment on a boring day. (Hey, it's 131 degrees! Wow, now it's minus 77. Celsius!) If I need to know the actual temperature, I can always listen to the deep voice of the guy on the radio. He usually tells the truth.

I sympathize with that poor little thermometer, because I have a faulty internal one of my own, attached to my emotions—those unreliable feelings that waver wildly out of proportion to reality, registering all sorts of exaggerated and imaginary dangers. When a trial produces even a little heat, my feelings scream at me that deadly global warming has arrived to roast our ministry planet. Any chill wind of personal rejection or icy drizzle of failure freezes my heart in a kind of passive panic.

My feelings are as misleading as our car's thermometer, because they don't reflect spiritual reality. Ministry trials by themselves can produce neither insufferable heat nor unbearable cold. The emotional boiling and freezing I feel are the faulty reactions of a heart that has forgotten to trust God.

I can't control how I feel. I'm a human, after all, and a woman besides. But I can control my thinking. Whenever I manage to marshal my disorderly thoughts and march them toward truth, my emotions follow. Whenever I discipline my mind to focus on the promises spoken by the deep, authoritative voice of God, my spirit settles down. When my mind is stayed on Him, my heart stops shivering and finds perfect peace. My wild emotional thermometer stabilizes when my heart is "fixed, trusting in the Lord" (Psalm 112:7).

I'm thankful to know that, because my emotional thermometer needs repair, even more than the defective one in my car.

44
While You're Not Looking

While this ministry mama wasn't looking . . .

— her toddler tore all the tags from the pile of gifts under the Christmas tree, shuffled them, and stacked them neatly on the kitchen table.

— the same adorable child explored her mama's purse while she was at the piano and dropped the week's grocery money into the offering plate.

— another precocious daughter wandered the pews following the Lord's Supper, removed the little plastic cups from their holders and licked them clean before putting them back.

— her busy little boy climbed into the pulpit after a service, picked up a live microphone and loudly sermonized, "All you people better get saved or I'm going to SHOOT YOU!"

I've decided not to tell you how this same mama stood her still-being-potty-trained toddler on a table in the church lobby for just a moment to re-tie her little shoe, and of the surprise yellow puddle that soaked the brochures, tracts, and missionary letters displayed there--because that would be too embarrassing.

But I've heard your stories, too, of platters of fudge mysteriously disappearing from church fellowships and of furtive swims in the baptistry. They make great family tales when enough years have passed to make them funny. In the meantime, it's good for a ministry mama to keep her eyes open, because strange things can happen when she's not looking.

That's not only true in your house and church. It's true in the spiritual world, too. While you're not looking, wicked old Satan is stalking like a ravenous lion, eager to swallow you up. He records your mixed motives, secret sins, and hidden hypocrisies, and they become his ammunition, as day and night he accuses you to God.

"Did You see what she did? Did You hear what she said? Just look at her cold heart," Satan sneers. "And she thinks she can serve You! She's a fraud, a fake and a phony. Why do You even love her? She's useless!"

His criticisms, if you could hear them, might sound familiar, for you have likely used them against yourself. And of course the sad truth is that he's right—none of us is worthy even to be God's child, much less to serve Him in ministry.

But—oh, the glory!—while you're not looking, Jesus Christ the Mediator speaks for you. He intercedes as your great High Priest, defending His sincere but fallible servant. He is your ideal Advocate, for He is your Savior. He shows His wounds, and as they fervently plead for you, the eyes of the righteous Judge turn from your fleshly failures to the precious cleansing blood of Jesus.

I cringe when I imagine what the old adversary is saying about me to the Father. Maybe he has accused me of allowing my children to become miniature vandals, thieves, and terrorists. I hope not. But whatever his awful accusations, I am immeasurably encouraged to know that while I'm not looking, Jesus my Savior is pleading for me.

45
Waiting for God

Why did Jesus make them wait so long? They were His friends. He had often stayed in their home, and we're told plainly that He loved them. Martha had served Him to exhaustion and Mary had sat adoringly at His feet. How strange it seems then that He responded so slowly to their cry for help. They had been sure He would come running, when with the confidence born of closeness they had sent Him this simple message: "Lord, behold, he whom You love is sick."

But Jesus, only a day's journey away on the other side of the Jordan, delayed His coming. When He arrived in Bethany—four very long days later—Lazarus was dead, and Jesus had missed the funeral. His sisters' gentle rebuke showed faith blended with disappointment: "Lord, if You had been here, our brother would not have died."

I'm not sure I would have been that composed. I know my impatience and frustration during my own waiting-on-God situations, even when the issues are far less critical than death. I find it terribly hard to handle His delays when I believe with all my heart that I have prayed in His will, that the answer would be for His glory, and especially when it's His work I'm doing.

"Why not?" I ask the Lord. "I know that You *can*, so why *don't* You? What are You waiting for?" Prayers that seem unheard and unanswered are my greatest test of faith. I suspect that I'm not alone in this, and that other Marthas and Marys of the world, when filled with more pain than faith, ask the same questions.

The problem is not with my eagerness for an answer or with my disappointment at His delay, but with the wrong conclusions I reach as my mind travels down a twisty trail of doubt. Maybe, I fret, He's too busy with more important people and issues to listen to me. Maybe my plea went unnoticed among all the other cries for help. Or maybe He did hear but doesn't love me or my ministry enough to answer. If I'm going to be ignored, I guess I'll just have to solve this puzzle, unravel this mess, fix these broken people all by myself.

Martha and Mary must have felt ignored, too, coping with awful grief while Jesus deliberately stayed away. The truth is, of course, that they were not forgotten by the Lord for even an instant, and neither am I. But He sometimes asks His children to wait, for His own good reasons. My purposes in prayer are often selfish—to have my problem solved, my pain relieved, my need met—but God's purposes are loftier than mine. He will work out His superior plans if I'll just wait.

Waiting enhanced the sisters' joy when the long-delayed answer came. Their brother's healing would have delighted them at any point, but coming as it did after every other resource was exhausted, after hopeful hours by his bed had ended in days of weeping at his tomb, their joy must have been overwhelming. Overwhelming enough to abbreviate the wait in their memory, and certainly enough to increase their faith tremendously when the next crisis came.

And I suspect that Martha and Mary's wait also purified their motives. Our first prayers in a crisis usually begin as an appeal for immediate relief. As days pass, by His grace our desires may become centered more on personal change, on asking God for grace to accept His will, whatever it is. Sometimes we even reach the ultimate selflessness in prayer: inviting God to glorify Himself even at the price of our own pain. That's what happened to Hannah, who began by praying for a child to satisfy her maternal yearnings and escape another's taunts. As time passed, though, her prayers were purified into longings for a son to give "unto the Lord all the days of his life." That change gave glory to Jehovah.

God's glory was also greatly increased by the delay in Bethany. Since Lazarus' body had been decaying in its sealed stone crypt for four days, no one could doubt that he had been thoroughly dead. This was no trick; there was no natural or circumstantial explanation for what happened. Since only God has power over death, Jesus was proved to be the Messiah. The delay confirmed the miracle, and the miracle, as miracles always do, brought God glory.

Why did Jesus make Martha and Mary wait so long? Not because He didn't care, for when He arrived, He wept with them. His delay was for their good and for His glory, and surely for one more very satisfying reason—so that you and I, while coping with His delays, can read their story and have hope.

46
Bargains

On a warm Wisconsin day, our family visited the Circus World Museum. We had seen somewhere an offer of free admission on that day in exchange for coming dressed as a favorite circus character. It was a bargain, and since we love bargains, our family of clowns merrily drove to the museum in mismatched clothes, bizarre hairdos, and painted faces. Sure enough, we all got in free.

We were barely through the gates, though, before discovering to our dismay that we seemed to be the only people in Wisconsin who had taken advantage of the museum's offer—and we had suddenly become a main attraction. We rushed to the restrooms to scrub our faces and repair our hair. There wasn't much we could do about our crazy clothes, but even in our weird outfits, we enjoyed the day, laughing at ourselves and ignoring the stares. After all, free admission was a bargain, and we love bargains!

A bargain is a large return on a small investment, a substantial benefit received at a low price. Our day at the museum was a bargain: we exchanged a little bit of personal dignity for a day of quality family fun.

Every ministry wife I know is an expert bargain-finder. She triples coupons and scours 75% off racks. She looks forward to half-price day at the thrift store. It's part necessity and equal parts challenge and fun, to see how far she can make the dollars stretch. But in reality, her whole life is a bargain, for she constantly exchanges the temporal for the eternal, the common for the extraordinary.

She gives up the security of a hefty weekly paycheck for the thrill of seeing a providential God miraculously meet her family's needs, from shoes and cereal to cars and college tuition. She exchanges a conventional 9-5, 5-day workweek, with vacations uninterrupted by other people's surgeries, for secure employment by a Master Who never makes a mistake or breaks a promise.

She yields the pleasures of frequent quiet family nights at home for the joy of being married to a man who responds compassionately to others' calls for help.

She forfeits the status of marriage to a prominent professional for the rare wifely privilege of being an indispensable partner in her husband's work. She gives up the comforts of living near relatives to receive an abundant measure of sweet oneness with her church family.

She trades her dream house in a country meadow for a narrow apartment in a congested metropolis, but the Lord transforms those city streets into her joyful harvest field. In exchange for privacy and anonymity, she becomes a daily model in her community, serving unaware as God's living pattern of joyful good works and kind words, of love, faith, and purity.

In return for her conscientious work, she expects no yearly bonus, regular promotions, stock options, or pension plans. Instead she cherishes the simple hope of someday receiving the only reward that matters: her Heavenly Father's "Well done!" On that day, she'll look back at her earthly ministry and realize that she actually never made a single sacrifice. Instead, her life will appear as one incredible bargain. And who doesn't love a bargain?

47
If You Knew

As far as Moses knew, his exile in Midian would last the rest of his life. If he had known it would end after 40 years, would he have found the back side of the desert less lonely?

If Sarai had known where she was going and for how long, would it have been easier to pack?

If Abraham had known about the ram already caught in the thicket, would it have been less heartbreaking to bind Isaac to the altar?

Joseph could not see an end to his slavery and imprisonment. Would knowing that he would be prime minister of Egypt by age 30 have brought light to his darkest days?

When Esther said, "If I perish . . ." she knew that death was a real possibility. If she could have foreseen the king's held-out scepter and the deliverance of her people, would she have wept fewer tears?

If during his deepest agonies, Job had known that Jehovah would bless him in "the latter days . . . more than his beginning," would he still have wished he had never been born?

Jonah knew he deserved his slimy swim in the fish's belly but not if he'd ever get out alive. If he had known he'd be free in three days, would the stink have been less stinky and the terror less terrible?

As far as the three Hebrew children knew, they were about to be burned alive. If they had known they'd emerge without a single blister, would they have entered the fiery furnace even more serenely?

As far as Peter knew, his denial of Jesus meant the end of his usefulness. If he had known what would happen when he preached at Pentecost just seven weeks later, would his bitter tears of repentance have been sweetened by hope?

If the disciples in Gethsemane had known what would happen in three days, would they still have forsaken Him and fled?

If you could see how after you have suffered a while, your trials would perfect, establish, strengthen, and settle you, would you find it easier to trust the God of all grace? If you believed with all your heart that your circumstances were working together to conform you to the image of His Son, would you thank Him for them now?

If you could foresee how the story of your adventures with God would someday encourage others in their own struggles, would that bring you hope? If you could read His end from your beginning as easily as you read these Bible stories, would you be encouraged?

"Wherein ye greatly rejoice, though now for a season, if need be, ye are in heaviness through manifold temptations, that the trial of your faith, being much more precious than of gold that perisheth, though it be tried with fire, might be found unto praise and honor and glory at the appearing of Jesus Christ: Whom having not seen, ye love; in Whom, though now ye see Him not, yet believing, ye rejoice with joy unspeakable and full of glory" (1 Peter 1:6-8).

48
Too Tired to Run

Too tired to run and too scared to stop—that was Elijah. The tired part isn't hard to understand. He had just humiliated and executed 450 false prophets and prayed so earnestly and fervently that a 3½-year drought ended. Then he tucked up his long robes and outran a king's chariot.

The scared part is understandable, too. After hearing death threats from evil Jezebel, the prophet ran again, this time into the scorching wilderness where he collapsed under the shade of a juniper tree. Exhausted and depressed, he prayed to die. An angel came in answer to his prayer, not to escort him to glory, but to provide what God knew he needed.

What did he need? Not more thrilling displays of Jehovah's power, not glorious visions and fresh challenges, not even exposition of scripture. He needed ordinary things: sleep and food. Stretched out under the tree, he took a nap. Soon a heavenly messenger woke him for a snack of angel-food cake. Elijah ate, rolled over, and took another nap.

Roused again by the angel and invigorated by more food, he set off for a Mt. Horeb retreat, where in a cave alone with God, he poured out his heart to the One Who always understands. "I have served Your people with all my heart," he cried, "but now I'm completely alone, and You're going to let me be murdered!"

Suddenly a strong wind split the rocks. The earth shuddered. A fire roared. But the Almighty was in none of these. Instead, He spoke gently as Elijah stood wrapped in his mantle, breathing fresh air at the mouth of the cave. "You're not alone," God explained, "and you don't have to deal with the wicked by yourself. I'll handle that job, and I'm sending you an assistant to help you do yours."

Maybe some morning you will wake up under a juniper tree with the same bone-deep ministry fatigue that Elijah knew—the spiritual exhaustion that follows both victories and terrors. When you find yourself too tired to run, don't be scared to stop. Do the simple things first: sleep and eat. Then find a quiet cave of your own where you can pour out your heart to God, releasing to Him the uproar of your emotions. Then breathe some fresh air and wait. In the quietness, you'll soon hear the still, small, encouraging voice of the One Who always understands.

49
Tie Her Up

No matter what you do, you can't please her. Anything you try that's new or different (different from what she's used to, that is) is bad. When you hear her voice on your phone, you grope for a chair, knowing her criticism will soon make you weak in the knees. Gossip and discord among the church ladies can usually be traced back to her voice on their phones.

She's an outspoken authority on everything from arranging the church kitchen to how long a sermon should be to *her* rules for rearing *your* children. No matter what the subject, she has an opinion, and you've noticed that it's usually the opposite of yours.

She'd rather grumble than help, but when she does accept a task, she expects extravagant praise from the pulpit. Because she's been around a little longer than you, she believes she's entitled—obligated, even—to correct you, and she might be genuinely surprised to discover how little you appreciate it.

If she were your employee, you'd fire her. But of course she isn't, and you can't. She's your sister in Christ, and you need to serve the Lord together—somehow! But she gets under your skin. The plain truth is that you don't like her, though you've really tried, are a little afraid of her, and sometimes wish you could just tie her up in a corner so you can go about serving the Lord in peace.

Well, go right ahead and tie her up! You can borrow my rope. It's a sturdy cord I found in I Corinthians 13. It's tested and guaranteed as the only way to make a friend out of an enemy. Here are some of its strands.

Attach a long fuse to your short temper. Bear with silent grace all slights, slurs, and snubs. Look for creative ways to bless her. Stifle your envy of her influence. Always regard her as your equal. Treat her with good manners. Sacrifice yourself for her good. Give her the benefit of the doubt. Look for things about her to praise. Refuse to stew over her faults or to recite them to others. Expect her to change, and in the meantime, love her. Love her, love her, love her. Bind her with resilient cords of Christlike love—the more, the better. Whenever she finds a new way to irritate you, toss out a new loop!

I know that's hard, because she steps on your toes, and sore toes hurt. So do stepped-on feelings. I haven't yet discovered out how to infallibly rule over my emotions. (When you figure it out, please teach me.) But with His help, you and I can control what we do, and love is an action—a chosen behavior rather than a feeling. Otherwise, the Lord's directive in Matthew 5:44 would be impossible: "Love your enemies, bless those who curse you, do good to those who hate you, and pray for those who spitefully use you and persecute you." Even if I can't control my feelings, I can choose to obey His commands.

While you're tying her up with love-cords, remember this: she's not the real enemy. That's Satan. You don't have to love him, of course. Just be aware of the sneaky tricks he uses to create ministry muddles and sore toes. And look forward to the day when the Lord is going to tie him up—not with cords of love, but with chains of eternal judgment. Until then, he'll be on the prowl, so keep your rope handy. As long as you're in the ministry, you're going to need it.

50
Blackberries

I've been out in the field picking blackberries this morning. You might have guessed that if you'd seen me walking home with my clothes smeared with purple berry juice and my hands covered with scratches. It's a labor of love to pick wild blackberries, because they are protected from predators like me by exasperatingly thorny branches. No matter which way I reach for ripe fruit, I encounter spiky spears that snag my clothes and jab my skin. Long before my bucket is full, I'm dreaming of going to the farmer's market to pick from its neat rows of already-picked baskets of berries. No thorns there.

But these are free, and somehow they seem sweeter for having survived in the wild. Or maybe I just enjoy enduring the perils of tackling an untamed berry patch and coming home bloody and triumphant to tell the tale. I do know that I savor the end results: icy smoothies, warm cobblers, and preserves heaped onto hot biscuits. The joy of arriving with a sweet harvest soothes the sting of those awful thorns.

Jesus knows all about thorns, for He wore a crown braided of them. He "endured the cross, despising the shame," for "the joy that was set before Him" (Hebrews 12:2). He is our ministry model. We need His example, because sometimes simply going to church can feel like entering a berry patch peopled with prickers. While struggling through them, you may find yourself longing for some easier way to make a living—one that doesn't involve thorns.

That's a good time to stand, stretch, and look over the patch to get some perspective. You'll discover that for every one thorny personality, there are plenty of other sweet friends who love you sincerely and serve Christ humbly. Each icky-sticky conflict is balanced by some other serene and uncomplicated relationship. The painful stings of ministry are nothing compared to the sweetness of seeing lives changed by the gospel that you shared, of being followed as you follow Him, of storing up treasures that you can take to heaven with you.

Thorns are native to blackberry bushes. That's Adam and Eve's fault. Instead of fretting because your berry bush has thorns, celebrate this: your thorn bush has berries! Don't fear or resent the prickers. They're just the signal that ripe fruit is close by. Press on, and you'll soon reach home with a full, sweet harvest.

51
Jumping Off Cliffs

I married a man who likes to jump off cliffs. David loves to take great leaps of faith, launching out into the unknown while trusting God alone. He lives life in bright red. Not me. By nature, I prefer to live in beige and avoid all risk. I'd just as soon stay behind the fence, far from any scary cliffs, and have a quiet picnic as I enjoy the view.

Whenever I see my husband staring at yet another precipice, it's instinctive for me to try to reason him out of it. But once he's certain that it's God's will for us, I know it's my wifely duty to follow. So I close my eyes, hang on to his faith, and take the plunge while wailing, "We are going to die!"

But we haven't died yet. In fact, every time I've expected to drop into an abyss, I've enjoyed a gentle glide onto the Solid Rock instead. There I've found peace, joy, and blessing--even a picnic or two—and felt deep gratitude that I married a man whose faith stretches my own.

The truth is that the fences I thought meant security were the walls of a prison instead—the prison of fear of the unknown, the fear of what others think, the fear of failure. Fear keeps ministry wives, and their husbands with them, in shackles. Fear impedes church planting and thwarts evangelism; it prevents the launch of bold new ministries and paralyzes progress. A fearful spirit is never from the Lord (2 Timothy 1:7).

It's the prison, not the cliff, that's the scary place. It's awful to realize that my female anxieties can hinder God's working through my husband. When His divine leading is clear to my human leader, it's time for me to stop digging in my heels and join him in bold strides of faith, not because my husband is flawless, but because it is God's work we are doing, and He's the One Who keeps us safe.

Every day, ministry couples stand together on the border of the Promised Land—the place of God's blessing waiting for those who will just trust Him and jump. His pledge is as true for a trembling wife like me as it was for the children of Israel: "Be strong and of a good courage, fear not, nor be afraid . . .for the Lord thy God, He it is that doth go with thee; He will not fail thee, nor forsake thee" (Deuteronomy 31:6). Even a coward on a cliff can be brave while clinging to a promise like that.

52

Ones

Follow Jesus' footsteps, one by one.

The disciples were hustling Him through a throng to the home of a wealthy man with a dying child when Jesus stopped for a conversation with one feeble, trembling woman who had just found healing in the touch of the hem of His garment.

Though thirsty and tired from travel, Jesus sat by a well and opened a conversation with one woman. This lonely Samaritan, rejected by the decent folks in her town because of her sin, became one of the first people Jesus told He was the Messiah.

The disciples believed toddlers too insignificant for Jesus to bother with, since they could do nothing to boost His kingdom. But Jesus gently held the sweet little ones, blessed them, and declared that they *were* His kingdom.

Prideful men poured money from their fat wallets into the treasury, but Jesus paid tribute to one woman who dropped only two mites into the box—a widow who had nothing to give but her all.

Jesus didn't spend the night in the home of a leading citizen of Jericho but called His host down from a sycamore tree instead. He didn't see Zacchaeus as the swindler he was, but as the new creation he would soon be.

Simon the Pharisee invited Jesus home to a Sabbath meal but neglected a host's usual courtesies. So Jesus allowed His feet to be washed by the tears, anointed with the perfume, and wiped with the hair of a public but pardoned sinner. He freely accepted the passionate worship of this woman who had scandalized the others by simply walking into the room.

While in the agonies of crucifixion, tormented by all the sins of all who would ever live, Jesus responded to the plea of a thief whose spiked hand stretched out toward His own. To that one penitent, Jesus spoke words of mercy and hope.

Though His disciples were close at hand and powerful priests and rulers nearby, the resurrected Jesus first appeared to one woman with a painful past—Mary Magdalene, once possessed by seven demons.

And I've watched you, too, focus on ones—little ones, lonely ones, poor, sick, scared, and scarred ones. Guilty, rejected ones. Uncultured and unsophisticated ones. Ones branded as irrelevant by the world but precious to the Savior. Others know how to work a crowd, but you know how to work with people, for you are an apprentice to the Master of all ministry, and you follow in His footsteps.

In His sight, that makes you one very special woman.

53
For Some People

For some people, church is optional—a nice place to go one day a week if nothing more interesting or urgent arises. Church is on the periphery of their vision, a sideline to real life.

Not for you. Church is the framework of your schedule, the hub of your wheel, the axis of your planet. You sacrifice your pleasure for its prosperity. You love your church as Christ loves His Church, and for that He honors you.

For some people, the pastor is the gray-suited man in the pulpit who is listened to until he's finished, greeted and hand-shaken at the church door, and called without hesitation night and day. Not for you. He's the man you married, fully human but fully His, a man who needs his dinner plate filled, his shirts ironed, his body rested, and his heart lifted. You protect him from schedule overload and strange women. You do him good all the days of your life. You praise him as Christ praises him, and for that Christ honors you.

For some people, prayer requests are jotted down and mentioned in a brief public prayer. They are granted one sympathetic murmur and then forgotten. Not for you. Prayer requests start your thought-train rolling. Who needs a phone call tonight? Can you make time for a hospital visit in the morning? Is there money in your purse to meet that need? Which family could use the casserole and pound cake stashed in your freezer? You care for the needy as Christ cares for them, and for that He honors you.

For some people, a low attendance at church is just a number. The absentees might be back next week. If they aren't, they aren't. Maybe somebody new will show up. If not, it's no big deal. Not for you. Every empty seat has a name and face attached, and you know them all. They may be sick or stuck in the snow; they may be offended and upset or just need extra attention. And you know that new folks will come only if you go find them and bring them in. You notice individuals as Christ notices them, and for that He honors you.

For some people, Christmas is a holiday. They come to church to enjoy stirring music and pageantry followed by a plate of homemade treats in a beautifully-decorated fellowship hall. It's their relaxing annual tradition. Not for you. Your holiday traditions include nightly rehearsals, frantic sewing of costumes, midnight baking of homemade treats, early morning decorating of the fellowship hall, and doing it all with joy. You serve as Christ came to serve, and for that He honors you.

You're not just "some people." You're one special person. You don't just look after people—you tend the Shepherd's sheep. You aren't building your own kingdom—you are serving the King of Kings. You aren't just busy—you're busy about His business. And for that, my extraordinary friend, I honor you.

54
Numbering My Days

The skeleton of a new year sits on the pages of my day planner. Jotted-in reminders of birthdays, anniversaries, appointments, and deadlines are its skinny bones. I'll fatten up the skeleton with the minutiae of life as days go by.

I can be certain of only one thing about my plans for this year: none of them are certain. I may scribble them in today only to scribble them out tomorrow. I'll have to alter my agenda and rearrange my schedule—sweetly, I hope—to accommodate others' needs. Surprises both blissful and dreadful will arrive. I may be with the Lord in glory (Glory!) by spring or celebrate my autumn birthday (Happy!) with Him. I will not make any big noises about any tomorrows, since I can't even know what today will bring.

There's another certainty about this year: I'm going to give account for every moment of it. Even a quick flip through last year's planner makes me miserably aware that too many of its days and labors did not count for eternity. I admit to my sorrow that I toted water past thirsty souls and hoarded bread needed by hungry hearts. Though I wore the label "full-time ministry" all year, I am dismayed at how little I accomplished that will endure, how often I squandered the wealth of hours I could have invested. This year, I intend to walk more circumspectly, redeeming the time, reminding myself every day of "how short my time is" (Psalm 89:47).

So I've decided on a January project: to record on each day of next year's calendar the number of days I've lived. Today, I've calculated, is about Day 20,894 of my life. (I know, I know, that's old.) It would be more motivating to record how many days I have left, but only the Lord knows that number.

This I do know: there is a God-determined limit to my days, and since I've already used up way more than half of them, I can't afford to fritter away even one more. By His grace, this year I will actively seek out the thirsty and hungry, and ripen ordinary contacts into redeeming relationships. I will treat each journey as a mission trip. I will be more concerned with keeping divine appointments than keeping to my schedule. I won't allow either the routine or the urgent to thwart the essential and eternal.

Maybe you'd like to join me by calculating and recording your days, too. Reading those big numbers on our calendars may be the sort of numbering of days that brings wisdom (Psalm 90:12). I hope so, because looking ahead at the coming year, I can see we're going to need it.

55
Only One Boss

It was an ordinary job, requiring little skill and few brains, so I was well qualified. Dan was my boss, and after he had explained my duties, I went off to work on my own, doing what he said to do. Before long, however, things got complicated.

Other employees began coming by with instructions that were different from those Dan had given me. These well-intentioned folks seemed confident in their authority and certain I would be glad to comply. I did make some adjustments, trying to please my self-appointed supervisors, but I quickly realized it was impossible. They disagreed with each other and contradicted Dan. There was no way to obey my boss and make everybody else happy, too.

I became so confused and frustrated that the next time a would-be-boss came by, I responded to him in an assertive voice rare to me, "Sorry. Dan is my boss. I'm going to do exactly what he says and nothing else."

In a huff, that man stomped off toward Dan's office. I felt uneasy and wasn't surprised when at the end of the work day, Dan spoke to me. "I heard that you said you're going to do what I say and nothing else."

I nodded, wondering as I did if I would soon be looking for another job. I was enormously relieved by what he said next: "Good for you. That's just fine with me."

I was as pleased as if I had heard him say, "Well done, thou good and faithful servant!" After that, I relaxed and enjoyed my work, confident that I was pleasing the only one who mattered.

I want to hear those extraordinary words of praise from my Master in heaven someday. I know you do, too. The only way for us to have that joy is to listen to His voice every moment and then do exactly, and only, what He says. That will please Him.

It may not please everybody else, though. People in your ministry, though they are just trying to be helpful, may make demands on you that contradict each other and exceed His expectations. If you struggle to satisfy people — all of them, all the time — you will quickly become confused and frustrated. Your ministry will be motivated not by love and joy, but by false guilt and needless fear instead.

Relax. Remember that like Paul, you are the bondslave of Jesus Christ, called and commissioned by Him as an instrument to bear His name in a specific place (Romans 1:1). The One Who once willingly made Himself a servant is not a demanding, unreasonable, or capricious Master. His commands are not grievous; His yoke is easy and His burden is light. Fear Him — but fear *only* Him.

If at the end of each day, you can stand before your Master's face with the confidence that you have followed His instructions, then you are a success. Like Jeremiah, you need not fear any other faces if He is pleased with you (Jeremiah 1:8).

You will enjoy a long-term, joyful ministry, and you can look forward to someday hearing Him say, "Well done, thou good and faithful servant!"

56
Fixing It

Okay, I admit it: I'm a fixer. The "as is" racks at outlets are my favorites, and mending is my favorite kind of sewing. I find it satisfying to all by myself make the useless useful again. If a repair is beyond my skill, I feel frustrated. I like being the fixer.

My itch to fix is a useful skill at home. Not so much in ministry, though, where instead of working with clothes, I work with real people with the flaws and failings, defects and deficiencies that come with being human. We all come "as is." I can diagnose others' problems with no trouble at all (much more easily than my own, of course), and I want to be the one to fix them, right now! The problem is that not many people want to be fixed, especially by me.

The Lord has been teaching me that repairing broken people is not my job. That's a very good thing, for how can I, with so many imperfections of my own, mend others? And what makes me think that I should even try to do the work the Lord has reserved for Himself? "I the Lord search the heart, I try the reins, even to give every man according to his ways, and according to the fruit of his doings" (Jeremiah 17:10). I'm slowly learning that when the Lord gives me insight into others' failings, it's not so I can criticize or change them, but so that I can love them and intercede for them with the One Who loves them most of all.

His diagnosis of their problems is always accurate, for "the Lord searcheth all hearts, and understandeth all the imaginations of the thoughts" (1 Chronicles 28:9). He makes His repairs from the inside out: "A new heart also will I give you, and a new spirit will I put within you: and I will take away the stony heart out of your flesh, and I will give you a heart of flesh" (Ezekiel 36:26). He can not only mend broken people; He can make them *want* to be mended. And the changes He makes are permanent. Any fixing I do is superficial and short-term at best—a flawed, temporary patching-up. But when God does His work in a human heart, it's transformed forever.

If I'll just quit meddling long enough to meditate on what He has promised to do, I'll stop feeling frustrated when people resist my most earnest attempts to change them. Instead I will joyfully turn over all repair work to the Master Mender, the One Who can fix anyone.

57
The Man I Didn't Like

Once upon a time, there was a man I didn't like. I couldn't stand him. Okay, now that I've confessed, I feel better. He had a sweet wife who was dear to me, but I never would have chosen him as a friend.

But there he was, a faithful, active church member, parked in his pew at every service. I was his pastor's wife, and I sat in a nearby pew, so I couldn't just pretend he was The Invisible Man. Outwardly I worked at being extra-friendly, hoping that he wouldn't realize that I found almost everything about him to be annoying and irritating. But inside I stewed, as frustrated with my awful attitude as with his exasperating eccentricities.

I knew it wasn't right for me to look at him through the dark glasses of ill will. I knew I should focus instead on his good qualities and appreciate the positive contributions he made to our congregation. But I couldn't come up with a single one.

I finally confessed my misery to my husband. "You're right," he agreed. "He's not likable. But why not decide to see him as an opportunity rather than a problem?"

What David explained to me in the next few minutes changed the way I looked at that man and has helped me ever since. He suggested that when I encounter someone so irksome to my natural self, I see it as an opportunity for the fruit of the Spirit to ripen in me.

After all, if nobody's unlovable, when do I get to love as He loves? If nobody ever upsets me, when does He get to pour His "peace which passeth all understanding" (Philippians 4:7) into my heart? If nobody pushes my patience to the limit, where's the need to demonstrate His longsuffering and self-control? If nobody's cantankerous, when do I get to witness His goodness, meekness, and gentleness flowing through me? And if nobody ever hurts and rejects me, when do I get to share in the fellowship of His sufferings?

I began looking across the pews through new glasses—not the rosy-tinted lenses of denial, but clear lenses that revealed him as an opportunity to be appreciated, not a burden to be borne. Gradually I even began to be thankful for him. He was good exercise. As I did, an odd thing happened. I began to detect, here and there, positive traits in him that had not been there before. That man had changed!

Or maybe—just maybe—that was me.

58
Taken for Granted

The day I walked headlong into the glass front door of the fruit market, I was glad the guys stacking melons spoke a language I couldn't understand. I'd like to blame the beautiful melons for distracting me from the big red PUSH sign on the front door, but the truth is that I just assumed it would magically swing open like most grocery store doors do. That door just sat there and let me walk right into it. I don't know which was hurt worse—my nose or my pride.

I no longer take automatic doors for granted. Now I notice them and say thanks. I should have done this a long time ago, since I'm a ministry wife and know how discouraging it can be to be taken for granted. It happens to us a lot, since most of what we do is never noticed. Don't be discouraged, my friend. I, for one, have been noticing you.

Those candy wrappers crammed into the crevices of the pew cushions—I watched you dig them out with your fingernail file. I saw you take the volunteer list after it had been passed around and sign up for every job not already taken. You're the one who pulled the dead blooms from the lobby lilies, updated the bulletin boards, and polished the piano keys.

The baptismal robes have been washed and re-hung in their closet, and there are fresh towels in the kitchen. I'm pretty sure you're responsible for that. I also happen to know that during Vacation Bible School you chose to teach the rowdiest class and brought extra cookies every day just in case someone else forgot. The church refrigerator has been emptied of dead leftovers and the cupboards of jobless families filled with fresh provisions. That's also thanks to you.

Sometimes, the thank yous are slow in coming, and you know that you are being taken for granted. Congratulations! To get to that level of service, you have to have been so faithful for so long that it never occurs to anyone that you might not do your job. You have to have been consistently reliable and trustworthy, serving without fanfare or reward and expecting neither.

Would you rather not be taken for granted? Quit doing your job for a while. Watch and snicker while people bump their noses on closed doors. Then they'll appreciate you!

But I suspect that that's not your style. You'd rather rest in the truth that "God is not unrighteous to forget your work and labor of love, which ye have showed toward His name, in that ye have ministered to the saints, and do minister" (Hebrews 6:10). I'm not the only one who notices you. The Father up above is looking down in love, and He never, never takes you for granted.

59
Monster IF

There's a monster living under my bed. His name is *IF*. He hides out during the day, but in the darkness of the night he slithers out and whispers in my ear. The sound of his ugly voice sets my mind to squirming by rousing the regrets and fears that I've been able to discipline away during the day.

His standard opening line is "*IF ONLY*," followed by a list of my failures. If only I had. If only I hadn't. If only I were. If only I weren't. If only I had said. If only I hadn't said. The monster *IF* leads a mournful parade of errors that leaves me littered with remorse and misery, for I know he is right about all this. I am only a sinner, after all, and sinners sin.

Then he moves from the past to the future. "*WHAT IF?*" he begins—and there's no end to the frightening possibilities that monster can suggest. Even without his help, once I'm awake in the silent darkness, I find it easy to imagine deep sinkholes down the road, dead ends and drop-offs lying in wait to doom our ministry and hurt people I love. Not all the dangers are figments of my groggy imagination. I know that some are real, though exaggerated by the darkness, and that they are rapidly approaching.

But that monster *IF* has a terror of his own—He's my Father, the Almighty God! As soon as I can gather my sleepy wits enough to call out His name, He rushes to my rescue. With His strong right arm, He drives away my personal ogre, and along with him the anxieties that have shattered my peace and stolen my sleep. Then rather than trembling under the accusations and insinuations of *IF*, I lie quietly listening to timeless, encouraging words spoken in the voice of the One Who cannot lie:

"*IF* we confess our sins, He is faithful and just to forgive us our sins, and to cleanse us from all unrighteousness" (1 John 1:9).

"*IF* God be for us, who can be against us?" (Romans 8:31).

"*IF* you walk in my statutes, and keep my commandments, and do them, then I will give you rain in due season, and the land shall yield her increase, and the trees of the field shall yield their fruit . . . . And I will give peace . . . and ye shall lie down, and none shall make you afraid" (Leviticus 26:3-6).

Meditating on such sweet *IFs*, I relax into sleep, and the monster, deprived of his prey, goes away — for a while. I'm not sure where he goes (though I do know who his father is). Maybe one of these days he or one of his nasty brothers will show up at your house. You might want to be ready, just in case. But don't be afraid. Your Father's *IFs* are bigger, stronger, and truer than any old monster's. Call out His name, and He will drive that ogre away.

60
Storms

The disciples were doing what He told them to do — no more, no less. "Get into the boat, and go to the other side," Jesus had said, and they had obeyed. So when a terrifying storm began as they reached the middle of the lake, they must have been as bewildered as panicked.

What was going on? Why would Jesus send them out onto deep water, knowing that just as they got to the farthest point from shore, winds and waves would threaten their lives? No matter how quickly they bailed or how vigorously they rowed, they were likely to die. Two tempests raged that day: one on the sea and the other in their hearts. I don't know which was worse.

I have never been in a storm on the Sea of Galilee, but I have felt like it, at least once. At a memorably low moment following a line of ministry squalls, I complained to my longsuffering husband, "This is a strange way for the Lord to treat servants who are just doing what they were told. Where has He gone, and why has He left us here to die?"

I was repeating the disciples' mistake of believing that I knew what God was up to. At Jesus' command, the disciples took off rowing, assuming that His goal was for them to arrive at the opposite shore. But His plan actually was quite different—to teach them something on the way.

He directed them into that storm to prove that He is the Master of tempests. He planted them in the middle of a tumult to demonstrate that He would always, eventually, come walking on the water.

We had embarked on a new ministry believing we knew what God was planning to do, that since He had called us to build a church, then big numbers, large offerings, and continuous victory were surely His will. But God's definition of success was not the same as ours. He wasn't just building a church; He was building us. His construction tools included storms that made no sense to us but perfect sense to Him. I thought our trying circumstances were hindering us from accomplishing His purpose, when they actually *were* His purpose, for His concern (as always) was not our comfort or success, but our character.

The disciples eventually reached the other side, but they arrived as different men. The Lord did build our church, but by the time the steeple was set in place on the first building, the ministry couple inside had been thoroughly changed. All that bailing and rowing had made us stronger. Sturdier, too, for we had learned to discern His face in the stormy skies. And suffering had made us softer, with ears freshly tuned to the panicked cries of other sailors floundering in their own gales.

Every storm is scary for us disciples in our little boats, but when we are there at His direction, there's no better place to learn from the Master.

(With a nod to Oswald Chambers)

61
Perfection

I give up. I can't do it. No matter how hard I try, I can't be perfect. And I can't imagine why I ever thought I could, since I have often read Romans 7:18,"For I know that in me (that is, in my flesh) dwelleth no good thing, for to will is present with me; but how to perform that which is good I find not."

But still I have struggled much too long for perfection in ministry, marriage, mothering, housekeeping, hospitality, looks, and relationships, believing that with enough effort, I could reach my impossible goal. Whenever I've detected my defects, I've poured buckets of self-reproach on my poor head, drenching myself with guilt. This is not a fun way to live, and it's not God's way.

It's true that 1 John 2:1 says, "My little children, these things write I unto you, that ye sin not," but then (hooray!) the verse continues, *"and if any man sin,* we have an advocate with the Father, Jesus Christ the righteous." Knowing that there would be people like me, the Lord says, "Don't sin. But since of course you will, here's a Savior for you."

What a relief! I can do my best without expecting to ever be The Best. I can calmly confess my faults to the Lord and to others (as though they didn't know them already). I can easily acknowledge my blemishes and admit the flaws of that woman in the mirror. I am looking forward to having some good laughs at myself.

The people in my little world are going to be relieved. Not only because I've finally come to my senses, but because now I'll no longer expect perfection of them, either. Criticism is such an easy task that once a critic finishes with herself, she has plenty of time to move right on to everybody else. But when she stops taking herself so seriously, she becomes generous with the imperfections of others.

Oh, someday, on the day He presents me "faultless before the presence of His glory with exceeding joy" (Jude 1:24), I'll be perfect. You won't recognize me then, because I'm finally going to be as flawless as I long to be—exactly like Him! Until then, I'm going to be content as my not-so-perfect but always-trying-to-please-Him self: "Not as though I had already attained, either were already perfect: but I follow after, if that I may apprehend that for which also I am apprehended of Christ Jesus" (Philippians 3:12).

Have you had backaches lately? Maybe they're coming from carrying around an impossible burden of perfection. I'm not surprised. It's a ministry wife malady. Dump it! It's much too heavy a load to carry, and the Lord isn't the One Who laid it on you. Let awareness of your own sin send you scurrying to the cross, not sinking into the Slough of Despond. The faithful and just One is waiting there for you, and He will be glad to see you coming.

62
You Know You're a Ministry Wife When . . .

Vacation Bible School is no vacation, and planning the church picnic is no picnic.

Easter and Christmas are not holidays, and Sunday is not a Sabbath.

After the ladies' retreat, you need one, all by yourself.

Going to funerals with your husband feels like a date.

Your husband has asked you to stop smiling so big at funerals.

You have prayed with a woman sitting on a hospital bedpan.

You recognize hymns by number as well as by name.

You're in the front row of the choir though you can't sing a lick.

When certain people offer to brew the fellowship coffee, blow up the junior church balloons, or turn on the baptistry heater, you show up early—just in case. With others, you don't need to. And you never forget which is which.

You slip into the pastor's office for a hug and kiss.

You listen for running toilets before you leave the building.

You're the one who always knows where the church plunger is.

You firmly espouse the doctrine of the Sunday afternoon nap.

You gladly give anybody your cell phone number, because you love people.

To have a day off, you have to leave your house without your cell phone.

Your work week runs from Sunday morning to Saturday night. Your vacation week runs from Monday morning to Saturday night.

On vacation, your family goes to "the shore," not "the beach."

You only dare to donate unwanted gifts out of town. Way out of town.

You're introduced more often by title than by name.

When people leave your church, no matter what the reason, you bleed.

You solve problems nobody else knows about.

About once a week, you talk your pastor out of resigning.

Your dinner table and your guest room are usually full.

Your ears, arms, heart, and kitchen are always open.

Your salary is only fair to middling but your benefits are out of this world.

You wouldn't have it any other way.

63
Aboard Ship

David and I like to explore tall ships, and the *Balclutha*, a 19th century square rigger, is a new favorite. When we poked around its captain's quarters recently, I felt very much at home, and I wasn't sure why. Maybe it was the compact, wood-paneled rooms, so much like the ones in our RV. Maybe it was my fondness for shiny brass. I was sure it wasn't the porcelain chamber pot.

Then I discovered, framed on the cabin wall, this passage from an old sea captain's book: "A captain's position on shipboard at sea is a peculiar one. . . . All on board, except himself, have companions; the crew have each other to talk with and confide their feelings to; the cook and steward fraternize; the first and second officers can confer, or even talk amicably together . . . The captain, if he has no companion, stands alone, isolated, in a certain measure, from all on board.

"Although he may converse with his first officer on all matters pertaining to the ship, and even unbend and talk about side affairs, yet he must never forget . . . the claims of his position in any way that might be misinterpreted or taken advantage of. . . . So, I believe, if the captain is married, and his wife is in good health, enjoys travel, and is not afraid of the water, it were better that she should accompany her husband on his voyages as one to whom he can always turn for companionship and confidences at sea. Woman's influence on shipboard, if she is a true, good woman, is felt for good throughout the ship . . . and there is certainly no place where more respect and courtesy will be shown her than on shipboard."

If I ever met a sea captain's wife, I would recognize her as a sister, for I too travel with my husband, on a lifelong voyage of ministry. Aboard ship, I help hoist and furl sails. I am a proficient polisher of brass and an experienced swabber of decks. But that's not why I'm along on the crossing. My commission is unlike any other sailor's: I am companion and confidante to the captain.

When I do my job well, my husband's "position on shipboard at sea" becomes less peculiar than pleasant. No matter how wild the waves or deep the deeps, he'll never feel alone with me standing by his side--hardy, happy, and resolutely pretending I'm not one bit afraid of the water. The truth is, of course, that I'd rather be moored in a snug harbor than tossed in a tempest, but even when I'm feeling sort of seasick, I'm still delighted to be with him on this passage. He seems to like it, too.

Somewhere out there, you—a true, good woman—are also accompanying your husband in his journey over wide seas. When your ship passes mine, shout "Ahoy!" We will smile and wave through our classy brass portholes, and then turn back to our wonderfully satisfying task of being an influence for good aboard a husband's ship.

(From *Life in the Old Sailing Ship Days* by Captain John D. Whidden, 1908)

64
Hill Climbing

Even now that I've grown up, the hill still looks steep. My grandparents' farmhouse was at the top, and at the bottom, Granddaddy's tin-roofed grocery store sat huddled between a curve and a creek. A gravel drive wound gently downhill from house to store, but whenever Grandmother asked me to fetch something she needed in the kitchen, I took the shortcut straight down instead, through the rails of the whitewashed yard fence and across a wide, flat ledge of rock. I hopped over fresh cow pies and dodged blackberry brambles as I galloped barefoot straight down the steep slope, all the way to the barbed wire pasture fence.

Across the dusty road, I'd pull from wooden shelves whatever Grandmother had asked for—a bottle of ketchup, maybe, while dodging Granddaddy's teasing. ("Cat soup? Why does she need cat soup? Our cats eat mice!") Loaded down with the ketchup and maybe a sack of sugar and a can or two of people soup besides, I'd start the climb back to the house.

The hill seemed a lot steeper going up, and I got tired. I always wanted to quit, but I never did. For one thing, I knew supper depended on me. And I had learned a trick that flattened the slope: I kept looking down. As long as I looked only at my next step, I didn't feel the steepness of the path or notice how far I had to go. I'd lower my chin and take one step, one step, one step at a time. Enough steps in a row and I'd be at the top, crossing the rock, scrambling through the fence, up the wide stone kitchen steps toward my smiling Grandmother.

My childhood climbing technique is still useful on morning walks and mountain hikes. It's even more useful when I stand in front of a steep mountain of ministry obligations with duties squatting solidly on my shoulders and uncertainties weighing heavily on my mind, when unsought but inescapable responsibilities have amassed into a hefty load and unwelcome changes that call for me to adjust and adapt have plopped onto my path like stinky cow pies.

When that happens, I'd much rather quit and sit, or turn and run, than press on. But I've discovered that if I will stop staring up the trail and lower my chin to focus on the task at hand (not a bad posture for prayer while I'm at it) and take one step, one step, one step at a time, before I know it, I'll have climbed even the scariest peak.

My welcome at the top is the smile of the One Who gave me strength sufficient for every step (Deuteronomy 33:25). And there I find it easy to praise Him, for looking back down the path, it's obvious that even with the help of my trusty climbing technique, that hill was way too steep for me.

65
Always the Same

The conversation lasted only about 15 seconds, but I have never forgotten it. I greeted a pastor friend at a ministry conference and asked about his wife. "She's fine," he answered. Then he paused as a grin spread slowly across his face. "She's the same every single day!"

What unexpected, unusual praise! I wondered at it through the service that followed. Of all the things a man in ministry might praise about his wife (beauty, hospitality, hard work), he chose her constancy. "The same every single day" — why would he set such value on that? Why did that compliment come so quickly to his mind?

Maybe because it's so rare. A woman, after all, is seldom the same two minutes in row. Our spirits sway with our circumstances. They can be flattened by small criticisms or sent soaring by the tiniest bits of praise. Since the ministry is a roller-coaster sort of life, a ministry wife has plenty of opportunities, and every excuse she could ever want, for her feelings to move up and down with it. Add in the stresses of home and children, not to mention those pesky hormones, and . . . pity her poor husband.

When he comes through the door at the end of the day, wearied by the minutiae of management, mind-numbed by hours of study, or drained by a day of rounding up wandering sheep, there's nothing he longs for more than the steady companionship of the sweet wife he kissed goodbye in the morning. But sometimes—right there in his very own kitchen—he meets the Wicked Witch of the West instead. He is bewildered by his quick-change artist of a wife and surely sometimes wishes she were more stable.

She can be, but not by herself, for stability is not innate or effortless for most of us female-type humans. Only in Christ is "no variableness, neither shadow of turning" (James 1:17). He is the solid, immutable Rock of Ages, and He can keep you stable.

When your earth quakes, anchor your thoughts to His unchanging promises. When storms roll in, hide in His shadow. When you're too tired to handle the demands of the day, let Him be the Rock of your strength. When your heart is unsatisfied, let the sweet water flowing from the Rock quench your thirst.

Whenever any scary or upsetting thing happens, run straight to the Rock. Climb on, settle down, and stay there. Your emotions will stabilize, your inner witch will melt away, and you (to your husband's delight) will become more and more like your Savior—the same every single day.

66
Mother

She and I were the original members of the Monday Morning Club. I was a young pastor's wife who often needed to unload to someone who understood what my life was like, and she—the only pastor's wife I had ever had—was always there to listen. She celebrated successes with me and reassured me during setbacks. She was my model, and she was a good one. For over six decades, she had lived at home what her husband preached from his pulpit. He had the ministry vision and set the course. With grace and steadfastness, she helped him make it work.

She loved the women in the churches he pastored, leading them to Jesus Christ and teaching them His Word, discipling them by godly example, loving them with thoughtful gifts and good counsel. When her husband left a large church in a compromising denomination to plant independent churches, she supported his convictions and with creative frugality stretched their income.

He brought in bushels of produce from his garden; she served it at countless family suppers and Sunday dinners, to guests ranging from lonely young servicemen to veteran missionaries. When her husband had a burden to begin a pioneer Christian school, she planned lessons, sanded and painted wooden blocks, taught with joy and energy, and then came home to cook supper, grade papers, supervise piano practice, and mother her three daughters. She ironed (her prayer time) and vacuumed long after dark. Somehow she found time to sew for her girls, even after all three had grown up and married preachers, and to earn her own long-delayed college degree.

Home and ministry never seemed to conflict. They gracefully overlapped. They meshed. Her husband's life was more fruitful simply because she was his wife. He knew that, and as long as he lived, he praised her to anyone who would listen.

Today I too rise up and call her—my own sweet mother—blessed. She never would have wanted me to tell you she was perfect, but now she is. She is in heaven with her Savior, and she is just like Him (I John 3:2).

I can no longer tell my mother how much I love her or how grateful I am for the example she set for me. So instead, I'm telling you.

"A woman that feareth the Lord, she shall be praised. Give her of the fruit of her hands; and let her own works praise her in the gates" (Proverbs 31:30-31).

Elizabeth Martha Horne Holmes
October 20, 1921 – February 7, 2010

67
Pleasing People

I knew our friendship was in trouble when she started acting aloof. She began skipping services and being openly critical, and before long she wouldn't speak to me at all. I wasn't surprised when I heard she was leaving our church family, but I was hurt and bewildered, with no idea what had made her so upset. When I finally did find out—secondhand—I was stunned. It was all my fault. At least she thought so.

She ordinarily sat in the back pew, in the corner opposite the piano bench I often occupied. I'm nearsighted, and though I didn't need glasses to see my music, everything beyond it, including the faces in the pews, was a fuzzy blur. Occasionally I'd look up to offer the crowd my sweetest pastor's-wife smile, but poor blurry-eyed me had no idea who in the world was out there. I could have worn my glasses, of course, but since I thought they made me look old and dowdy, I didn't.

My friend in the opposite corner had been smiling, nodding, and waving to me, but I had acted as though she were invisible (which to me, of course, she was). She stewed at the insult, then tried again and again with the same result until she boiled over. Her anger toward poor innocent, oblivious me grew into bitterness toward everything about our ministry.

When I learned what had happened, I tried to make things right, but no explanation, apology, or plea of ignorance could ever win back her friendship. Solomon spoke the truth: it's easier to conquer a fortified city than to appease an offended sister (Proverbs 18:19).

The whole episode was humbling, painful, and terribly guilt-inducing, but (as such things usually are) full of useful lessons. Right away I scrapped my stupid vanity and put on my glasses. Then I focused on this encouraging thought: other friends in the pews, whose smiles, nods, and waves I also had unintentionally ignored, had not taken offense. They gave me the benefit of the doubt, and just because they loved me, chose not to feel snubbed or insulted. Or maybe they had just heard the silly thing about my glasses.

But what helped me most of all was finally accepting this absolute reality of ministry: I cannot please all the people all the time. No matter how hard I try to be Mrs. Perfect, no matter how careful I am to avoid intentional insults, somebody, sometime, is going to be offended by what I do. Or don't do. Or can't do. Or didn't know I did. Or never even heard of anybody doing.

If I think my task is to keep every person in every pew happy, I'll stumble through ministry in a sort of passive panic. But that's not my job. People are here for me to love and serve, not fear.

I still miss my long-lost friend. But when I think about her these days, it's with more gratitude than grief, for the Lord used her to teach me some lessons I really needed to know. Even without glasses, it's easy for me to see what He was doing.

68
Eavesdropping

A power struggle was going on at the church my dad pastored. I was only a teenager watching from the sidelines as the conflict unfolded, but even I knew that it was pride and hypocrisy that were destroying our church's peace and harmony. As my parents walked through those painful days, I watched them carefully, searching for any cracks in their façade of godliness, any sign of pretense in their professed love for God and people. If I could spot any hypocrisy in my parents, I decided, then I could rebel, and it would be their fault.

I listened to what they said and (even more significant) *didn't say* about those who had declared themselves their enemies. I heard them respond gently to some awfully cranky people. And I heard them pray, both in family devotions and kneeling together by their bed at night. Those late night private prayers weren't meant for me to overhear, but when their quiet voices carried into the hallway, I stood near and listened, knowing that if they were bitterly complaining to God about their circumstances or calling down lightning from heaven to devour the wicked, I'd hear it when they were praying alone.

But that's not what I heard at all. Instead I heard compassion for the cantankerous, submission to the Father's will, pleas for quick deliverance from the trial, for patience and wisdom in the meantime. Not much different from their prayers with the family at the supper table. Just more tearful, more fervent, and a lot longer.

Many years later, after my husband and I had been through several ministry crises of our own, I thanked my mother for their example during those difficult days and for the overheard prayers that became a model for me. She listened as I quoted some words I had heard them pray and then responded quietly, "Well, Claudia, all I can say is that you must have done a lot of eavesdropping."

She was right. I was an eavesdropper, not just on their prayers, but on their lives. As I watched and listened to my parents, I discovered plenty of imperfections, but no hypocrisies. They were too real to give me any excuse to rebel against the truth they taught me. And when life later brought me the same sort of trials it had brought them, I tried to respond the same way they did.

If you're in a ministry battle right now, you may be worried that your children may be among its casualties. No need to fret—conflicts are inevitable in their lives, too, and they need to know how to handle them. The best way to teach them is by your example, and the best way for them to learn is by eavesdropping.

69
The Easy Way

Even after I had tried every recipe in every one of my cookbooks, my biscuits still didn't taste like the ones I remembered from summer mornings in my grandmother's kitchen. In my memory, they were perfect, and nothing else would do. When I finally asked my mom if she knew her mother's secret recipe, she laughed a long time before answering, "Claudia, those were *canned* biscuits."

I was shocked. This was the grandmother who raised ten children on a mountain farm, gardening and canning to feed them, sewing through the night to clothe them, and quilting by hand to keep them warm. By nature and necessity, she made everything from scratch. Except, it seems, biscuits for a horde of hungry grandchildren.

The more I thought about it, the more I understood. There were a lot of us, and we woke up early and starving. She always promised that if we would pick blackberries without complaining, she would make sure we had warm jam for breakfast. And blackberry jam just begs for biscuits. I can't even imagine how many we devoured. Now the whack of a can of refrigerated biscuit dough on the edge of a kitchen counter takes me back to her kitchen and reminds me of what she taught me by example: sometimes it's okay to do things the easy way.

Every ministry wife I know works hard. I'm sure there are lazy ones (if that's you, stop reading here), but I've yet to meet one who isn't diligent to the point of exhaustion. She knows her job has eternal significance, so she's determined to do it right. But I've noticed that the most relaxed and joyful ministry wives, the ones who wear well over the long term, are the ones who have learned that sometimes it's okay to underdo, understate, and uncomplicate.

It's hard to do that without guilt. I remember feeling terrible the rushed evening I served visiting missionaries KFC chicken, instant mashed potatoes, and both peas and biscuits from cans—on paper plates. But when I realized that my memories of a relaxed supper and sweet fellowship had long outlasted my guilt, I developed the courage to simplify in other ways.

I re-played offertories and left bulletin boards bare. I changed our formal ladies' tea into a picnic, and stiff weeknight bridal showers into relaxed after-church fellowships. Monthly ladies' meetings with agendas, officers, and committees were swapped for informal gatherings with volunteer help. Some folks didn't even notice; those who did, seemed relieved. We discovered together, as our stress levels dropped, that simpler is nearly always sweeter, and that some traditions hold more trouble than value.

What matters of course is not programs, but people. Just as sweet as her biscuits with jam was my grandmother's spirit as she plopped them onto our plates. Her recipe didn't matter, but her relaxed attention did. Maybe it was precisely because she made biscuits the easy way that she had time to sit and smile at us across the breakfast table.

If your church is still at the simple-by-necessity stage, enjoy it while it lasts! But maybe this morning finds you standing nose-to-nose with a complex, demanding church calendar, and you feel weary as you foresee months of frantic dogpaddling through details. Sit down today and bravely, prayerfully, decide where and how to simplify. Believe what this grandmother learned from her grandmother a long time ago: sometimes it really is okay to do things the easy way.

70
Looking Up

My voice shalt Thou hear in the morning, O Lord; in the morning will I direct my prayer unto Thee, and will look up (Psalm 5:3).

"Keep looking up!" When I was little and heard my daddy say those words, I thought he meant that we should be watching for Jesus to return. And we should. But as a young wife calling home long distance from our first ministry, I began to hear his words as this sound advice from a ministry veteran to a novice: when you need to be encouraged, *up* is the only sure way to look.

Instead of looking up, you probably will look around first, to the sweet friends the Lord has sent to work with you. But even the best of people are just people, and they will eventually disappoint, even when you're truly not expecting more of them than they can deliver. They can't help it. They're sinners just like us, and frankly, they may not even know what it is you expect them to do or to be.

You could look back instead of up, and sometimes that's a good idea. Your ministry may not be where you want it to be, but it's probably a little farther along than it used to be. Look at the past to see how far you've come. But if you stare backwards too long, you may discover that your glory days are behind you, unlikely to return. Or you'll see that your progress has been just as tedious and the road just as steep as it seemed. And the path ahead is . . . well, it's no wonder you're feeling tired.

You could look inward, of course, and be encouraged by how much you've grown in wisdom, humility, and faith. But you're likely to also see dregs of doubt you thought you'd left behind, anxieties you were certain you'd outgrown, impatience you hoped your trials had cured, inconsistency, hypocrisy, coldness of heart, envy, and--oh dear, that's enough of that.

By this point you may be looking down, head hanging in discouragement, face drooping in despair. Stop it and look up! Look up to see your Savior smiling down on you. Unlike all others, He is entirely trustworthy. "There hath not failed one word of all His good promise" (1 Kings 8:56). He can do "exceeding abundantly above all that we ask or think" (Ephesians 3:20). He is "the same yesterday, today, and forever" (Hebrews 13:8).

Let go of the past, with its triumphs and tragedies. Tackle today with confidence in His promises, and press on in faith toward tomorrow (Philippians 3:13-14). Ignore your inadequacies to focus instead on His perfections. Your spirit will rise, your heart will lift, and your miseries will melt away.

"Keep looking up!" My dad had said that so often that when a few days before he died, after speech had mostly left him, he looked straight at me and pointed upward, I knew what he was trying to say. It's good advice for you, too. Keep looking up!

71
Interruptions

The candy she kept on her desk was my excuse to drop by, but I was mostly interested in her ears, for she was a great listener. She'd turn away from her computer screen to focus on me, laughing and nodding at all the right places, treating me like a welcome reprieve from her endless duties as a church secretary.

I had never really considered that I could be anything else until the day I overheard her pastor praise her. "She helps me," he said. "Interruptions annoy me when I'm trying to 'get ministry done,' but she reminds me that interruptions aren't hindrances to ministry. Interruptions *are* ministry."

Oh. So I wasn't a delightful interlude in her otherwise dull day. She was ministering to me, loving me by listening, no matter how much she didn't get done while I loitered by her desk. Come to think of it, I did always leave her office refreshed, and it wasn't just because of the candy.

After that, I began to interrupt her less and watch her more. I saw her read to a toddler while his troubled parents prayed with the pastor. I listened as she graciously answered yet another phone call from yet another lonely shut-in. I watched her skillfully solve the most absurd problems of the most ridiculous people and shield the pastor from pushy peddlers. By treating her schedule not as a tyrant but as a guideline, she was free to welcome whatever or whoever the Lord sent not as irritations but as gifts from His hand. Unexpected company was just another way of watching God work out His best plan for her day.

I never did figure out when the bulletins got printed, prayer lists updated, and financial statements posted. When did she stuff letters and answer e-mail? I do remember surprising her late one Saturday night in the church office, her hair in curlers—but mostly she just seemed to work her magic on her paperwork as easily as she did on our hearts, dispensing love and encouragement as freely as candy from her dish. She coped equally well with paper and with people, but it was obvious which was her priority.

Are you annoyed this morning by the wrench some monkey has thrown into your careful plan for today? Relax and remember: interruptions aren't hindrances to ministry. They *are* ministry.

72

Fish Fry

New friends had invited us to what they called a "fish fry," so I dressed the way any girl from the South would dress for catfish, hushpuppies, and pitchers of sweet tea set on a picnic table. But we weren't in the South anymore. When we arrived at the address we had been given and were offered valet parking for our Volkswagen bug, I knew I was in trouble.

Fish fry? It was no such thing. It was a gourmet seafood buffet in an elegant setting—china, crystal, string quartet, and all—and everyone but me had known to dress up. Way up. Our friends quickly forgave my fashion faux pas. At least they seemed to get over it much faster than I did, and it did give us all something to laugh about. But a new pastor's wife living in a new place wants to do everything just right. I still wince when I remember being so badly dressed.

After that I learned to ask more questions, and so far I've managed not to repeat that exact mistake. But more often than I'd like to admit, I've been a poorly-dressed ministry wife, clothed in garments entirely unsuitable to my calling.

That's not the Lord's fault. The day He took me as His own, I gave Him my filthy rags and put on Christ instead. Since He's faultless, I ought to be always perfectly turned out. But sometimes, without planning to, I slip back into my wretched, stinky rags. Temper, resentment, envy, fear, egotism, and deceit slink out of a secret closet in my heart and slither onto me before I even notice. Yikes, those clothes are ugly — and sometimes I even wear them to church!

Others may not notice (hypocrisy's a handy cover-up), but I know without doubt that I'm badly dressed and that it's certainly nothing to laugh about. The Lord's not impressed with my ensemble, either. It's not just unsuitable; it's hideous. And prickly and uncomfortable besides.

I can't wait to change, and I don't have to. Even in the middle of the church lobby, I can turn to my Savior and by His grace swap the ill-fitting works of darkness for the armor of light. Suddenly I'm dressed just right — in the tender mercy, kindness, humility, meekness, and longsuffering that are always in style for a ministry wife, entirely appropriate for every occasion.

What did you wear to church yesterday? If the answer makes you cringe, don't despair. The Giver of all good gifts will gladly provide perfect garments. Whether it's to church or to a "fish fry," you and I can always be dressed exactly right.

73
Magic Ears

The trouble with Jenny's ear was that she could hear not only what people were saying, but also what they were thinking. Jenny's story was one of my favorite growing-up books. Back then I desperately wanted one of her marvelous ears and brothers like hers who would use their dictionaries and encyclopedias to help me win spelling bees and piles of money from quiz shows. I'm wiser now. You and I both know that we're much better off not knowing what people are thinking.

I thought about Jenny and her amazing ear when I stood in front of a group of women who had just said goodbye to a pastor's wife they had loved for a long time. Their faces were so sad that I couldn't go on with the class without asking, "Why did you love her?"

They looked puzzled for a moment, and then someone offered, "It was her ears. She knew how to listen."

Heads nodded all over the room, and then another added, "Once I went to her house weighed down with a burden, and when I left, it was gone. When my husband asked what she had said to help, I realized that she had hardly said a word. She just listened. She had magic ears!"

They weren't magic, but they were rare. Talkers are plentiful; listeners are few. It's an exceptional woman who absorbs more words than she dispenses. But any woman who wants to help others has to learn to be quiet, for a heart cry can be heard only in stillness, and deep pain surfaces only in a silent place. Even without an ear like Jenny's, when it's quiet enough you can hear the most important words of all — the ones not spoken.

Sometimes all that's needed to heal a wounded soul and lift a sagging spirit is one loving listener. For at its core, listening is love, love that sacrifices its need to be heard in favor of hearing, its desire to lecture in favor of learning, its opportunity to show off in favor of showing compassion. Instead of always leading the way, a patient listener, just by nodding in all the right places, can help a wanderer discover the right path on her own.

Quiet listening requires no aptitude or training, but it does take self-discipline to be "swift to hear, slow to speak" (James 1:19). Try it. Practice. You'll find the effect on your personal ministry even more marvelous than Jenny's ear. You may never win spelling bees or piles of cash, but someday you too will be heaped with loving praise for those magic ears of yours.

(*The Trouble with Jenny's Ear*, Oliver Butterworth)

74
What Somebody Said

I think I know what somebody said . . .

—when the palsied man was lowered through the roof to be healed: "We ain't never done it that way before."

—while picking up 12 baskets of leftovers after the 5000 were fed: "What a mess!"

—when Jesus gathered little children into His arms: "Don't You have more important things to do?"

—when He called for self-denial and cross-bearing: "Sorry— that's not my style."

—when He chose the unlearned and ignorant to be His disciples: "They're not part of our target demographic."

—when they heard Jesus was a Nazarene: "He's from the wrong side of the tracks."

—when He announced that the last would be first: "That's not fair."

—when He honored a widow with only two mites and sent a rich young ruler away sorrowful: "He ought to cultivate friendships with wealthy donors."

—when Jesus allowed a woman to anoint His feet with her tears and wipe them with her hair: "Why can't He be more dignified?"

—when He taught truth by telling stories: "His preaching is shallow."

—when He talked with the woman at the well, when He ate with publicans and sinners, when the common people heard Him gladly: "He attracts riffraff."

—when Jesus took only Peter, James, and John up the mountain where He was transfigured: "He's playing favorites."

—when He accepted worship and forgave sins: "Who does He think He is? God?"

—when He was crucified: "What a failure."

And if you and your husband have been hearing similar words lately, I think I know what Jesus is saying to you: "Well done, my servants. You're starting to look like Me."

75
Damage

Of the thousands of prospecting phone calls we have made while planting churches, it's the one I remember best. To my question, "Are you actively involved in a local church?" her answer was a quick and curt *no.*

I followed up with, "We are mailing out information about a brand new church. Would it be okay if . . . ?"

She broke in, her voice cold, "I am a damaged ministry wife. Church is NOT in my future." Click. She hung up. I should have called back to offer to talk, to listen, to do something — anything — to help her. But I didn't. I just didn't know what to say.

She came to mind recently when I heard a weatherman offer his advice about preparing for an approaching hurricane, "Remember: damage is easier to prevent than to repair."

To every ministry, storms come, and (praise be!) they go. Most are fast-moving local squalls, but some are more like hurricanes — terrifying monsters that threaten major harm and seem interminable. There's no way to avoid all storms, but it is possible to prevent the kind of damage that scarred the heart of that lady on the phone.

Of course, when you see a storm building, you could evacuate, leaving the ministry entirely for some easier way of making a living. But that doesn't sound like you. You are committed to serving Him by loving and leading His sheep, no matter how ornery. So you stay put and face whatever comes.

Instead of abandoning your post, you and your husband hunker down with your emergency supplies: the solid truths of God's loving sovereignty and the old familiar promises of the Word that shine so brightly in the dark. You secure the shutters of your faith, hang onto each other, and ride out the gale on your knees, believing that He has allowed it to come, will limit its scope, and will bring it to an end.

It's too late for me to call that lady back, and sadly, I suspect it's too late to help her. Damage is easier to prevent than to repair. But you have time to get ready for your own storms. Stock up on truth, right now. Store up His promises in your head; hide them away in your heart. They will sustain you no matter how sudden or long the tempest.

When the skies finally clear, you'll emerge to fresh, sweet peace in your world and in your heart. You won't have merely survived; you will have grown into the mature faith that comes only from seeing God prove Himself true. And the next time you see scary thunderheads rising, you'll remember that

> The clouds ye so much dread
>
> Are big with mercy, and shall break
>
> In blessings on your head.
>
> — William Cowper

May many joyful, storm-free days of serving His church be in your future!

76
The Dump

At our Tennessee house, we don't have garbage pickup, so instead of one of those big plastic trash bins with wheels, we have a corner in the garage where stinky bags of garbage can sit quietly as they wait for a lift into town. After a few days, the *eau-de-rubbish* wafting from the bags reminds me to load them into the trunk of the car and head for the city dump.

The dump has a more sophisticated name, of course. Sanitary disposal site? Eco-friendly recycling center? Refuse refuge? I really can't remember. Only the town-council-persons use its proper name. The rest of us just call it the dump.

I think it deserves whatever fine name it was christened with, because it's one of the nicest dumps I've ever had the privilege of visiting. It's impressive in a small town sort of way— clean, with an oddly sweet smell. There are neatly-labeled bins for anything anybody would ever feel like dumping. It's arty, too, with colorful towers of cubed, compressed soda bottles hovering over squiggly rows of dead kitchen appliances. The combination of sculpture garden, dumpish Stonehenge, and cultural comment is fascinating.

But my favorite place at the dump is the general household garbage compactor. Sometimes a friendly helper trots over with a cheerful, "Can I help you, ma'am?" (valet service at the dump!), but I really like to do this myself.

I pop the trunk and with a few mighty swings toss my stinky bags up, over, and into that giant green monster machine. Whoosh, thump, and the garbage is gone, never to be seen again, at least by me. I'm not sure what happens to it next. I can't imagine who would want it. But I do know that I love the freedom of the moment I drive away with no more trash in my trunk and no more stink in my nose. What a relief!

That's how I felt at the end of one very dark night following a day filled with bad news—news I had reacted to with every negative emotion ever invented. I had tossed and turned in bed for a while and then moved to the couch to wallow in—okay, I admit it—self-pity.

I could give you polite words for what I was feeling ("justifiable concern" comes to mind), but that's rubbish. No matter what happens, a beloved child of the Sovereign of the universe has no excuse to allow that much faithlessness, fear, anxiety, bitterness, and self-protective anger to rot in any corner of her heart.

I held a counseling session with myself, the kind I've held with other women. After a painfully honest conversation, I turned from my sin toward the Savior, and the One Who is "good, and ready to forgive, and abundant in mercy" (Psalm 86:5) took the garbage right out of my heart. Suddenly it was gone, never to be seen again. I know where it went, by the way—to the cross to be covered by His blood (1 John 1:7), as far away as the east is from the west (Psalm 103:12), down into the depths of the sea (Micah 7:19). With a clean and peaceful heart, I went back to bed and to sleep. What a relief!

Sometimes when the trash bags are not terribly stinky, I have been known to load them up, do my other errands in town, and totally forget to drop them at the dump. When I get home and have to set the bags back in the corner of the garage, I don't feel one bit smart. But I'm determined that I will never, never again let those grubby sins back into any corner of my heart. Even I am smarter than that. At least I hope I am. I fervently hope I am.

But just in case, whenever you notice I need it, feel free to remind me to visit the dump. I'll do the same for you. Hey—maybe we'll meet there someday!

77
Point Loma Pause

It only happens when we're visiting our friends in southern California, and only outdoors. We're chatting away to a background of rustling palms, singing birds, and the muffled hum of traffic on its way to the Pacific when abruptly—literally out of the blue—an enormous fuel-heavy jet loaded with vacationers and their luggage lifts off from the nearby San Diego airport. Its shadow blocks the sun, and its growling, deafening roar paralyzes the conversation.

They call it the Point Loma Pause. It lasts only about 18 seconds, but it happens a lot. The first time you experience it, it does give you pause, but after a while, you don't look up anymore or even think much about it. The Pause is a fact of open-air life in that gorgeous place.

The last time we were there, the Pause became my friend. The conversation stopped as usual, but by the time it ended, I had decided not to say what I had been on the verge of saying when it started. Instead I (whew!) detoured toward words that were kinder and more loving, more hopeful and positive, better in every way than I had planned. It's amazing, the good that can come from waiting even 18 seconds before letting words fly.

There are pauses like this in the Bible. They're called Selahs—musical notations that gave Psalm singers a break to rest their voices. Selahs also gave the players of timbrels, harps, trumpets, organs, and psalteries time to breathe and re-tune their instruments. It was a moment of silence, not awkward and involuntary like the ones in Point Loma, but a welcome break.

These short and simple Selahs gave the congregation and musicians time to *"think about that!"* They offered time to consider rich truths like God's sovereignty and justice, His righteousness and holiness, His providential control over every detail of life. Right in the middle of their song, the people stopped to think about the God of the music.

If you keep the music of your days playing loud and fast without any scheduled Selahs, you'll always be out of breath. Others will be jarred by the sour notes coming out of your mouth. You'll be off-key and out of sorts—flat when you need to be sharp, sharp when you should be gentle, fake when it's better to be natural. These are cues that it's time for a Selah, signals that it's time to take a few deep breaths and re-tune your heart.

Pausing even 18 seconds to remember His loving providence over a quaking world can head off panic. If you stop to focus on His longsuffering before you hit "send," you're likely to reword that e-mail. Eighteen seconds spent recalling His lovingkindness to you will increase your patience with other wandering sheep. A short break to remember His justice will blunt your passion for personal vengeance. Focusing on His omnipresence will lessen your loneliness. Taking frequent Selahs to turn your mind from your temporary crises to His eternal truths will keep you singing strong all day long.

When I'm outdoors in Point Loma and have something I
have to say *right that minute,* the short Pause can seem
awfully long. I want to raise my voice and press my point
over the sound of the roar. How foolish to be so impatient. If
it's worth saying, it can wait 18 seconds. And how silly to
react impulsively to the circumstances the Lord allows in my
day without taking even that much time to look up to Him
first. Pauses may be small moments in the song of a
woman's life, but they make a big difference.

Selah — think about that!

78
Frozen Shoulder

Leaves from the oaks around our house had fallen knee-deep, and we had only one day at home to make them disappear, so the five of us jumped in (literally) and got to it, raking, piling, and burning leafy heaps until the job was done. Leaning on my rake in the twilight, watching the last wisps of sweet-smelling smoke rise through bare branches, I was overwhelmed with satisfaction.

And fatigue. And when I woke in the night, with pain. I had overworked the underused muscles, ligaments, and tendons in my right shoulder, and it hurt. It really, really hurt. Over the next few days, I tried every pain reliever in our medicine cabinet, but my shoulder still ached. Poor me. Every movement hurt.

So I stopped moving. I bound my arm tightly in a makeshift sling and did not use that sore joint. I became a lefty and didn't ask my right arm to help me out at all. It worked! After a while, I was free of pain and congratulating myself on my self-doctoring skills—until I took off the sling and discovered that I could no longer raise my right arm higher than my shoulder. It didn't hurt anymore; it just wouldn't go. No matter what I did, it wouldn't budge.

One trip to the clinic, and I had a diagnosis: adhesive capsulitis, or more simply, a frozen shoulder. It took several painful and painfully expensive trips to a therapist to get the thawing started, and weeks of at-home exercises (including the use of one particularly gruesome pulley device) to break down the adhesions and get back full use of my right arm.

And it was all so unnecessary. Well, the leaves did have to be raked, and too much work done too fast was bound to result in pain, but the freezing-up part didn't have to happen. As the therapist explained, I should have kept my injured joint moving. Gentle motion in spite of the early ouches would have healed it quickly. Pampering my pain is what caused my long-term misery.

Because I coddled my aching joint, it froze. And injuries to your heart will freeze your spirit if you don't work through them. Allow your mind to dwell day after day on what some thoughtless person said or did, and you'll soon find yourself stuck in a sort of ministry paralysis, frozen by the fear of more pain. You'll withdraw into throbbing self-pity instead of pressing on with what you're called to do.

People are people, and until we have something better to work with, we're stuck with them. (And they with us.) Ministry wives who thrive long term are the ones who have learned to smile their way through small injuries, loving and serving people regardless of their response, knowing that the more unselfishly they spend and are spent, the more they become like the Savior (2 Corinthians 12:15, Colossians 1:24).

Those who flourish in the Lord's work are not free of pain. They just don't bind it close to their hearts and allow it to harden there.

So when those inevitable hurts come, keep pressing on. You'll stay warm-hearted and flexible, a useful tool in the Master's hand. Frozen people aren't of much use to Him.

And by the way, by the next raking season, we owned a leaf blower. What a marvelous invention!

79
Abba

Do your family members have special nicknames for each other? We do. They're a sort of verbal shorthand for communicating love, instant reminders of our family ties. They keep us connected when we are apart. They sound the sweetest when we hurt, for they convey a tenderness that soothes aches, heals wounds, and calms fears. They are hugs spoken out loud.

We aren't eager to tell strangers our nicknames. You might tell us they sound silly (and you'd be right). If you join our family, you can use them. You'll probably even get one of your own. But until then—sorry, but those names are private. Family names are reserved for family.

That's what makes this verse so amazing: "Ye have received the Spirit of adoption, whereby we cry, 'Abba, Father'" (Romans 8:15). Believers are encouraged to call on their Father with the intimate term "Abba," a family name used by young Jewish children, the same name Jesus used when He prayed to His Father in the Garden of Gethsemane.

Picture Him in the garden. Sweat mingled with great drops of blood as He prayed alone. Behind Him was betrayal; before Him was the cross. Shuddering at the terrible trial He was facing, "sorrowful and very heavy" (Matthew 26:37), He poured out His heart to His Abba-Father. Then, in surrender to the Father's will, He rose and headed for the cross.

Because He died on that cross, you can join God's family. And then as His child, you receive the family privilege of calling on Him as your Abba-Father, Who cares about every doubt, every fear, and every hurt of His child. You don't have to cower as a slave or approach Him timidly as a stranger but can come boldly, with confidence in His affection for you. When you are filled with distress, in your own place of private pain, you, like Christ, can call out confidently to your Abba-Father.

Why should the God of the universe care that much about you? I can't explain His love, but I can assure you that it is yours to enjoy. You could never earn a place in His family, and you don't deserve such family privileges. But they are unquestionably yours. How glorious it is to have them, and how sweet to use them!

Are ministry burdens weighing heavy this morning? Do you need your Abba-Father? He is eager to hear you call out His name. After all, you are a cherished member of His family. Use and enjoy your family privileges.

80
Mother Love

I'm not sure when I first began to feel like a mother. Maybe it was when I heard the doctor's voice on the phone telling me the test was positive—I was pregnant! Maybe it was while I walked around moaning with nausea and waddling with baby weight. Surely those hours of labor had something to do with becoming a mother. Or maybe it was the first time I looked into my daughter's deep blue eyes. I do know when I first felt the heavy responsibility of motherhood. My newborn was seven days old, my own mother had just left for her home 800 miles away, and for the first time that fragile pink person was absolutely dependent on me, an amateur!

I was terrified, but somehow we both survived, and as she grew, I grew, too, into a woman who could no longer think of myself apart from her. She was never out of my mind, even for a second. Her tiniest whimpers of hunger woke me. One clap of thunder in the night sent me running to check on her. Her needs took precedence over mine. She not only moved into our home; she moved into my heart.

She is still there, nestled beside her sister and brother. They are no longer babies, but I'm still their mother, and as soon as my eyes open in the morning, my thoughts fly around the world to each of them. As long as I am alive, my love will embrace the ones I carried in my womb. I delight in them. I intercede for them. I simply *can't* stop thinking about them, for I'm their mother.

The endurance of a mother's love is astonishing. But even the most affectionate mother is fallible. Isaiah asks, "Can a woman forget her nursing child and not have compassion on the son of her womb?" and then answers, "Surely they may forget. Yet I will not forget you" (Isaiah 49:15). I can't imagine how a mother could ever forget her nursing baby, but it is sooner to happen than for the heavenly Father to forget you. Every need you have, however small, is His concern. He longs to calm your fears. He holds you in His heart and intercedes for you. He thinks of you night and day.

Ponder the intensity of a mother's love. Multiply it by a million, and that's not even a fraction of the Father's passion for you. You are His delight. He never forgets you, even for a second. He *can't* stop thinking about you, for He's your Father.

81

Another Angel

I met another angel! Just like the last time, it was at a tough time and in an unlikely place.

I had been stumbling through a long, painful day, leaning hard on three scriptures the Lord had led me to in the early morning. I was quoting them to myself while shopping at Wal-Mart. As I turned into the paper goods aisle, an older woman in a motorized wheelchair rolled slowly toward me. She stopped, looked up at me, and asked the most unexpected question: "Are you a nurse?"

When I shook my head, she followed up with, "A teacher?" I shook my head again.

"Actually," I answered quietly, "I'm a preacher's wife."

"Oh, praise God!" She softly clapped her wrinkled hands. "I knew it! I knew you were somebody special! You serve our Lord! Oh, glory, glory, glory!" The warmth in her deep, velvety voice touched my aching heart.

I knelt beside her chair and looked into her dark, compassionate eyes. "Yes, but sometimes it's hard. Our hearts are hurting today and . . . ." I couldn't say more and couldn't stop my tears from spilling over.

She took my hand, and her tears flowed with mine. "Oh my dear, my dear, I know all about pain. It hurts. It surely does hurt. But oh, it's our chance to grow. Our chance to die. Our chance to see Him prove His promises true. Do you remember these?" The lump in my throat grew as I listened to her quote the three unusual passages the Lord had given me that morning—the very ones I had clung to all day to keep me from drowning.

"And sweet one, someday real soon, you and I are going to see His face right up close, and then none of this is going to matter one little bit! Bless your heart. You can trust our wonderful Lord. Let me talk to Him about you right now." And there in the aisle, as I knelt beside her, she prayed for me.

I hugged my new old friend. We talked a little more and agreed to meet in heaven and remind each other of where we met. And just like that, my encounter with an angel was over. It would add drama if I could say I looked back and she had disappeared. Maybe she did, but I didn't look back. I picked up a package of napkins and walked on, my eyes still swimming with tears but my heart lifted.

Was she an angelic being sent to the paper goods aisle at Wal-Mart? I don't know about that, but for me, she was an authentic angel, for she was God's messenger of truth, a courier of love to His hurting child. Our meeting didn't mark the end of that trial, and there have been hard days since. But whenever I feel despair descending, I stop to remember the love on her face and the warmth of her words, and it's like getting a hug from God.

Would you like to see an angel? Look in the mirror! For wherever you are, my ministry friend, you notice people. You perceive their pain and act as God's messenger of hope. The Lord puts you right where you're needed most, and you don't let Him down. I'm glad, because aching people like me need angels like you.

The other angel? I met her in the hallway of a doctor's office in another city at another difficult moment, and she was wearing an old-fashioned nurse's cap—but that's a story for another day.

82

Cemeteries

It's a pastime that sets me up for lots of teasing, but I still like to wander in cemeteries. I'm intrigued by tombstones — the older, the better. Epitaphs used to be some sort of final admonition to the living, like the classic "Prepare to Follow Me." But modern tombstones tend to be unemotional records of names and dates. I enjoy searching for the ones that are different.

Sometimes they make me laugh. In Mississippi, the deceased's address is carefully engraved below his name: "RFD 2". Was he expecting mail? A Wisconsin man wanted his epitaph to tell us that he has just "Gone Fishin'." In North Carolina, an elderly preacher is buried shoulder-to-shoulder with his wives, all three of them.

Other times they make me think. On a late fall afternoon, I discovered a fresh, elaborately-carved pumpkin on the grave of a ten-year old girl who had died many years earlier, on October 31. In the deep South, I read this poignant inscription on the tombstone of a young father, "All Our Hopes Lie Buried Here." In Alabama, I sat a long time by the grave of the aunt I was named for, staring at my own name engraved on a tombstone.

Whenever I enter a cemetery, I am gripped by the truth that each marker represents a human soul who lived, loved, and labored; who created, cried, and celebrated. Each one, with all the details of his life, was fully known to God. I catalogue the deceased as we do in life: male, female, rich, poor, young, old.   But God's one-word epitaph for every tombstone would read simply *Saved* or *Lost.* In life, every individual chooses which his will read.

As I walk out through cemetery gates, I celebrate knowing as my Savior the One Who has conquered death. Death holds no sting for me! And I praise Him that He lets me spend my life serving Him. Because He has called me to ministry, I can devote my days to helping change future epitaphs from *Lost* to *Saved.* I'm overwhelmed at my privilege. After all, what else really matters?

Maybe someday I will be walking through a cemetery and stroll by your grave. I'll read your epitaph and wonder about you. But of course you won't be there. You will be forever with your Master. And in heaven, I promise, you won't remember any of the sacrifices of ministry. You will instead be overwhelmed with gratitude that He let you spend your life helping to change other people's epitaphs.

83
Acorns

Maybe you saw me that windy afternoon as I crawled around gathering acorns, tossing them into a brown paper bag. If you did, you probably wondered if I had finally lost what was left of my wits or morphed from ministry wife into oversized squirrel. Don't worry. I was gathering those cute little nuts for an object lesson. And while I was on my knees on the damp ground, the Lord taught me one.

As I scooped hundreds of acorns from their cozy nests of fallen leaves, I looked up into the oak's spreading branches and felt like apologizing. These were the mother tree's babies, her hope for the next generation. She had dropped them onto the ground hoping they would find fertile soil, sprout, and grow up beside her.

But I knew that no apology was necessary. She was a mature oak, after all, so she knew that if every one of her acorns grew into a tree, there would soon be thousands of trees impossibly crowded around her roots. She never expected all of them to grow.

So why work so hard at producing acorns? Because she knows some of them *will* grow. If she drops just one acorn, a squirrel or a nut like me might come along and steal it. But if she drops thousands of them, some will sprout. A few will develop into baby trees, and one—maybe just one—will endure to become another tall oak.

Her job isn't to insure their survival, though she provides her leaves as cushions, fertilizer, and shade. She just does her job sowing abundantly right where she lives. How many grow and survive is the Creator's responsibility.

Sometimes it seems that the ministry involves too much sowing and too little reaping. We drop gospel seeds in many hearts, but few respond. We teach Bible truths over and over, but many don't hear, don't believe, don't apply, and don't change. It can be terribly discouraging unless we remember this: our job is to sow abundantly and nurture lovingly. It's the Lord's part (and His promise) to give fruit that remains. Some of those seeds *will* grow. Success lies in the sowing, not in the reaping.

My leafy friend didn't look a bit discouraged. She stood tall and strong. She had done her part, so she was a success. I left with a bag heavy with her acorns and with a heart made lighter by her lesson.

84

Church Classifieds

Wanted: a gardener. The flowerbed by the church front door is sprouting dandelions.

Wanted: a custodian. The soap dispenser in the ladies' room is empty.

Wanted: a secretary. The weekly bulletin has to be formatted, printed, and folded.

Wanted: a program planner. The hymns listed in the bulletin need to be chosen.

Wanted: an editor. No errors can appear in that bulletin.

Wanted: a decorator. The hallway is dull and bare.

Wanted: a painter. Bathroom walls are dingy.

Wanted: a cook. Teens are hungry for pots of chili and plates of brownies (frosted, please).

Wanted: a counselor. A woman is threatening to strangle her husband.

Wanted: a model. Ladies need a pattern of modest dress.

Wanted: a child-care specialist. A toddler is throwing a tantrum in the nursery.

Wanted: a hostess. Missionaries arrive Saturday afternoon.

Wanted: a friend. Somebody is lonely.

Wanted: an arbitrator. Personalities in the pews are clashing.

Wanted: a flower arranger. Pulpit posies are drooping.

Wanted: a landscaper. Somebody needs to grow fresh posies.

Wanted: a promoter. Visitors must be visited.

Wanted: a truant officer. Absentees need to be rounded up.

Wanted: a substitute. The junior high boys' teacher has a splitting headache.

Wanted: an event planner. The Annual Ladies' Extravaganza is in six weeks.

Wanted: a costume designer with a glue gun. Christmas angels need gowns, wings, and haloes.

Wanted: a chauffeur. A widow needs a ride to the doctor.

Wanted: a comforter. People get sick and go to the hospital. Sometimes they don't get well.

Wanted: a pennywise purchasing agent. Choirs need music. Copiers need paper. Teachers need flannelgraph figures.

Wanted: a switchboard operator. The phone is ringing. And ringing. And ringing.

Wanted: a listener. Needy people are calling.

Wanted: a wife. The pastor's not complete without one.

Flexible schedule. Weekend work required, especially Sundays. No age or educational requirements but must love people and be capable of delegating tasks. Servant's heart a must; smiling face a bonus. No wages; eternal benefits guaranteed.

Wanted: a woman to "serve the Lord [and His church] with gladness."

Wanted (and needed): YOU!

85

Attics

I've been busy cleaning out my attic. I decided to do this while I was helping my parents move from the house they enjoyed for many years. For several days I crawled around in the cobwebby corners of their attic, bumping my head on rafters, peering into long-forgotten boxes, and thinking about attics.

If you're like most people, your attic holds mementos of happy days and souvenirs of special events--and a plethora of junk. Anything you're not quite ready to toss goes up the ladder, out of sight and out of mind, until the attic is so crammed that you have to face reality: you've accumulated a pile of useless stuff, and you've got to get rid of it. As you clean and sort, you'll be astonished at what you find. Why did I keep that? What made me think this was important? Why didn't I toss that a long time ago?

Since I live in an RV and RV's don't have attics, I can't hang on to much junk. But I'm working on attic clean-up of a much more personal nature—ridding the crannies and cubbyholes of my mind of clutter and debris. My brain holds memories of cherished friends, valuable lessons learned, and answered prayers. I'm keeping those treasures. But lots of garbage is up there, too, and it's time to dump it.

Junky fears left over from a painful experience have caused me to dread the future (after all, it could happen again). The rubbish of a bad first impression has made my spirit dark toward another believer. The garbage of injustice has left me with lingering bitterness. The litter of gossip has made me suspicious. A thoughtless comment has caused resentment which I have hoarded, though it's trash that should have been discarded long ago. I wonder, as I stare at this mental garbage: why did I think this was worth keeping? Why did I cling to it?

I've clung to it, of course, as a fleshly response to difficulties my sovereign Lord allowed. I've tolerated it in disobedience to the command of 1 Peter 1:13 to "gird up the loins of [my] mind." But I'm determined to save garbage no longer. By His grace, any thoughts that are not "true, honest, just, pure, lovely" (Philippians 4:8) are going straight to the dump where they belong. To store them anywhere else would displease the God Who "searcheth all hearts, and understandeth all the imaginations of the thoughts" (1 Chronicles 28:9).

I'm delighted that cleaning up my mind won't involve moving any more heavy cardboard boxes. I'll be bending my knees, not my back, in a sincere prayer of confession and repentance, and His blood will cleanse my unrighteousness.

In my parents' attic I uncovered the chronicles of their long, fruitful ministry and mementos of the growing-up years of their three daughters (including the flawed middle one). Nothing shameful or dishonorable was stored in their attic. Let's do our best to keep the rubbish out of ours, too.

86
Reaching Home

She was only about 8, but that's old enough to use an IPad to talk to a dad who's been deployed to the other side of the globe. Perched on the living room couch, feet tucked under, she squinted through the screen at his fuzzy image, bit her lip, and asked, "Daddy, where are you?"

I couldn't hear his answer, but she echoed the last few words, "You're . . . you're . . . in the GARAGE?" Her eyes opened wide as her daddy stepped into the living room, still in combat fatigues, phone still at his ear. One flying leap and she was in his arms, weeping and hugging as though she would never let go. Daddy was home!

I was in tears. I wasn't there in person, nor do I even know that soldier daddy and his daughter. I was watching a cell phone video of a surprise homecoming being broadcast on the news. I can't even fully relate to the scene since my daddy never went off to war.

But I have felt like that little girl on the couch, talking to Someone I love through a blurry screen. Though prayer is one of the most precious privileges God gives His children, communicating with Him can seem as awkward and difficult as though He were not near as breath but on the other side of the universe instead. At its best, prayer is still "through a glass darkly." And when His voice is muffled by self-imposed distance or the cloud of circumstances, I have even been known to ask, "Father, where are You?"

How often I have longed to talk to Him unhindered by the static of the world or the frailty of my flesh, with no barriers of time or space or doubt, face to face, knowing as I am known.

That day will come. Maybe this morning He will come through the clouds and you and I will see Him in the same blink of an eye! Or maybe He will call my name and take me home. Either one would be an even more blissful moment than that little girl's daddy walking into the room. Better than any homecoming surprise could ever be.

The Lord, of course, won't be the one coming home from war—that will be me. My battle will be over, my wounds healed, and my enemy banished. I will have fought my fight, finished my race, and kept my faith. His explanations will be clear to my ears and His providence plain to my eyes. I will be at home with my Abba-Father. No strenuous climb of good behavior will have gotten me there--just one simple step of faith in the blood shed for me.

That sweet hope keeps me pressing on. There's a great day coming, and even though I have no idea when it will be, He does. He has it marked on His calendar for my life, and He is looking forward to it as much as I am.

This day is His gift to me, a day to serve Him with all my heart right here where I am. But that one is going to be the best day ever—the day my Abba-Father gathers me close, never to let me go.

87
Preacher's Kid

I was a preacher's kid. I watched my parents garden and can, sew and mend, scrimp, save, and make do. We had less stuff than some of our friends. But when I watched my dad in the pulpit, I could see that he thought he had the best job in the world. And I learned that there are more important things than money.

I was a preacher's kid. The day Daddy came out of his home office with a lady who had just accepted Jesus as her Savior and asked to borrow my globe so he could show her how her sins were removed as far as the east is from the west, I saw his face shine and his eyes glisten, and I learned why he loved his job.

I was a preacher's kid. When famous and not-so-famous preachers came to town, we cleaned and cooked on Saturday so we could bring them home for Sunday roast beef. They smiled and teased and took off their shoes, and I learned that though they were our honored guests, they were also real people, and I could trust them.

I was a preacher's kid. Sometimes grown-ups came over after the Sunday evening service, too late for little girls to stay up. Mother sent us to bed, but we stayed awake and waited under our quilts because we knew she'd come with goodnight kisses and Coke floats in little glasses on a tray. I learned that even when our parents' duties took them away from us for a little while, we were never out of their thoughts.

I was a preacher's kid. Even when I squirmed through morning prayer and Bible reading, eager to ride my bike or finish my Nancy Drew or cram for a test, Daddy made sure our family began each day by giving it to God. And I learned to put Him first.

I was a preacher's kid. No errand with my dad was ever quick, because he was always stopping to talk to folks, to learn their names, hear their stories, hand them gospel tracts, and ask if they were saved. On those errands I began to see people as more than clerks and waitresses and attorneys and mechanics and nurses and mailmen. I learned that every person is a soul Jesus died for.

I was a preacher's kid. When a grown-up scolded me for something I didn't even do and added the stinging, "And you're the preacher's kid!" I marched indignantly straight to my parents, certain they would take up my righteous cause. But when they just smiled and said gently, "We're sorry, Honey; people are like that," and dropped it right there, I learned that some things aren't worth fighting for, and pride of reputation is one of them.

I was a preacher's kid, and when I saw my dad give up friendships, position, and pension for the sake of defending the scriptures, I learned that some things *are* worth fighting for.

I was a preacher's kid, and I once heard my dad at his desk asking God to help, guide, and bless a man I had just seen storm out of his office, slamming the door behind him. My father prayed as though praying for a friend, and I learned what it means to love an enemy.

I was a preacher's kid. When I grew up to be a preacher's wife and called my mother to cry about a problem and said, "But this never happened to you!" she laughed a little and asked, "Don't you remember when . . ." and I didn't remember—not at all—I learned that preachers' kids can be shielded from what's happening outside their happy home. And that's a good thing.

I was a preacher's kid. When I hear that a church or a school my parents started is growing and thriving, or when I come across folks they led to Christ long ago, and they love me now just because my parents loved them then, I learn what it means to reap blessings someone else has sown.

I was a preacher's kid. If you want to learn what's important, there's no better way to grow up. I'd like to tell your children that, but they're not here right now. Why don't you tell them for me?

88
Impossible Job

Most jobs call for a specific set of skills, but a man in ministry needs them all. He needs to be:

A student of ancient languages, eschatology, hermeneutics, ecclesiology, soteriology, and apologetics who can communicate what he knows to a 6-year old.

The CEO of a corporation with a totally volunteer labor force.

A man of vision who can also manage details.

A father whose children recognize him in the pulpit, since he doesn't put on a different face along with his Sunday suit.

A man who gives himself for his wife as Christ gave Himself for His church. Their two smiles are the only ones that matter.

An adult with several degrees content with the salary of a teenager with none.

A shepherd willing to sacrifice anything, except his family, for his sheep.

Quick to run to comfort another's broken heart but content to run to God alone with his own.

Able to carry weighty burdens without allowing them to crush his spirit.

One who can live above reproach but be a true friend to those who don't.

Both a prophet to rebuke sin and a priest to dry the sinner's tears.

One who walks in the light so he can help the ones wandering in the dark.

Able to serve meat and milk from the same spoon at the same time.

A servant who knows he has only one Master, and how to deal with those who think they're Him.

Truthful but tactful, tough but tender, calm but fervent, firm but flexible, dignified but relaxed.

Shepherd, preacher, evangelist, administrator, counselor, financial manager, writer, referee, recruiter, organizer, motivator, and educator. Frequent chauffeur, proofreader, and song leader. Occasional gardener, janitor, and emcee. May also be expected to be a mindreader.

This job is not just hard; it's impossible! These men have rejected the notion of career for a calling that requires them to walk on water. And they make it look not only doable, but enjoyable. I give heartfelt thanks for these men, and for you, too, my friends, who more than anyone but God will ever know, make their impossible job possible.

89

Jeremiah's Wife

He was set apart to serve the Lord before he was born. Just as his ministry was beginning, God warned this 20-something novice preacher that his work would be 2/3 negative (uprooting, smashing, destroying, overturning) and only 1/3 positive (building up, planting). Prepare yourself, God said, because it's going to be tough. Kings, priests, and ordinary folks will be furious with you every day for the rest of your life. They'll fight you. They'll hate you. But I'll take care of you, and I'll put my words in your mouth. Just be my spokesman.

And that's what he was. He said everything God told him to say, preceded by, "Thus says the Lord!" And sure enough, it was a tough life. His family rejected him; his hometown friends despised him. He endured unjust trials, painful floggings, and near-starvation. He was locked into chains and stocks and threatened with death by murderous mobs.

He dictated long messages from God to one loyal friend who read the scrolls to the people, who reported them to the king, who sliced each scroll into fuel for his fire. Dungeons were his regular lodgings, but even they were luxurious compared to the muddy cistern where he was once lowered to live in suffocating filth.

Enough to cause some discouragement, don't you think? And he did get depressed. He once longed to run off to a desolate shack in the wilderness, far away from the mocking shame of his daily life. But the Word of the Lord burned in his bones and he couldn't abandon his call, so he stayed put and pressed on, for 50 years.

It would have been hard to be Jeremiah's wife. When a man's ministry is opposed, the wife faces a double-whammy: the sting of personal rejection plus the ache of seeing someone she loves suffer. During those five decades of ministry, Jeremiah's wife wouldn't have had many pain-free days. Maybe not even a single one.

So when God advised him not to get married, He was, as always, wise. But if Jeremiah had had a wife, and I could talk to her, here's what I'd say: look past your pain to God's purposes.

Look at what He is doing *through* your husband, not just at what He allows to be done *to* him. He is God's chosen mouthpiece to speak truth even when he's afraid of the people who need to hear it.

And look at what God is doing *in* your husband. Those tears you see when he's discouraged come not from self-pity, but from compassion. They are the overflow of a heart of love for people. A tough exterior with a tender core — that's a weeping prophet, and that's a man God uses.

And it's a man He comes close to. That long-ago preacher, so bold before other humans, was humble before his Lord. The hard circumstances of his ministry squeezed sweet, sad poetry from his soul, yet right in the middle of his most profound lamentations, in confident faith he suddenly sang,

"His compassions fail not! They are new every morning. Great is Thy faithfulness!"(Lamentations 3:23).

If he could sing those words at that time, in that place, then when you're asked to taste a bit of suffering you can sing them, too—even if you're not Jeremiah the prophet, but Mrs. Jeremiah instead.

90
Standing Ovation

The crowd rose to give a standing ovation in tribute to the pastor on the platform. I watched his wife stand and applaud along with the rest of us as we honored him--for work I knew *she* had done.

It's true that the vision had been his. He had prayerfully determined God's will, established the objective, set the course, rallied the troops, and led the charge, but she had directed the details, handling many of them herself and skillfully delegating the rest. Without her, his dream could never have become reality. No one else would have had any idea how to keep up with their energetic leader as he strode down the road toward the goal.

But because of her, the work was accomplished, the problems overcome, the goal reached. And now her husband was being honored for *her* job well done. It didn't seem fair. She deserved at least half that applause. Surely she (and he) knew that!

I searched her face for any sign of resentment, but it wasn't there. No discontent, anger, disappointment, or sadness, either. Fatigue showed up, of course, but not one bit of frustration. What I read on her face instead was satisfaction with a huge task finally completed and delight with the acclaim being given her husband.

As I got to know her better, I began to understand why her husband hadn't called her to the platform that day. Even the smallest word of public thanks made her blush. She simply loved her husband and their ministry and wanted them both to succeed. When they did, she didn't care who got the credit. In fact, she was always surprised to be told that she had anything to do with it and sort of embarrassed that anyone else would think so.

As more time went by, I discovered something else. In private, her husband gave her all the lavish praise that he shielded her from in public. He knew how perfectly suited to him she was. His vision was panoramic; she focused on details. While he gazed way past the present into a future no one else could see, she was making a list of what needed to be done right this minute. Where he saw a forest, she saw trees with small branches and tiny leaves. He planned the itinerary; she packed the suitcases.

Without her, he could not accomplish all he could imagine. He easily and gratefully acknowledged her worth as his perfectly-designed helper and friend, a priceless gift from a wise God. His heart safely trusted in her; he knew no fear of spoil. And he also knew that the one thing she didn't crave was public praise.

But I would like to give it to her anyway. The problem is that she's not going to recognize herself. Models of meekness are like that. So if you're reading this and think I couldn't possibly be talking about you, chances are that I am.

While nobody else is looking, step up onto the platform and smile sweetly as I admire and appreciate, congratulate and commend you. Try not to blush. It won't take long, I promise. I just want to offer you a private standing ovation for a job very well done.

91
The Desert

Come with me to the desert. We'll drive through shimmering sunlight along a flat, straight highway. The scenery that was so striking at sunset is dreary at noon, a panorama of drab beige. Dusty green sagebrush, spindly creosote, and spiny cacti blend into a desert camouflage. But suddenly, in a low wash, we spot a tree. Not a mirage or a tall cactus—a real tree! We can't help staring. It's startling, and we're curious. How can a tree survive in this arid place?

The answer is obvious. Water is nearby, somewhere. Long ago, a seedling sprouted and sent its roots down to drink from an underground stream. It grew into a tall tree, with its sturdy trunk and branches still satisfied by its hidden source of moisture. Its leaves absorb the sweet water and stay green.

Rolling down the road in our air-conditioned car with a cooler of iced tea, we're not tempted to dig for that stream. But if we were parched pioneers trudging across this wasteland, we would. We would be more than curious; we'd be desperate to find and drink from the tree's source of life-giving water.

Maybe you serve the Lord in a dreary desert, a place of spiritual drought encircled by shriveled souls and barren lives, by withered and wasted people who have turned away from the sweet water of truth to live in a parched wilderness of lies. Lives that could be fruitful are sterile instead as they try to satisfy their thirst at Satan's salty springs. They drink and drink of what the world calls pleasure, but there's no quenching of their cravings. Instead their longings increase, and they don't know that what they are actually yearning for is the God Who can fully satisfy, Who can take a life that's withered and bring life where there was death.

And there you stand, like a flourishing green tree in the middle of a desert. Your roots have sunk through Satan's dry sand to drink from the sweet water of God's Word. In the midst of deadness, you are alive. Even when pressed by life's harshest winds, you are stable. You don't shrivel in the heat of trials. You are like "a tree planted by the waters, which spreads out its roots by the river, and will not fear when heat comes, but its leaf will be green, and will not be anxious in the year of drought, nor will cease from yielding fruit" (Jeremiah 17:8).

Like a green tree in the desert, you attract attention. You're different. Of course, not everyone who notices will stop to ask about your secret source of life. Most will speed by with only an apathetic glance. Others will gape at the oddity of you and wonder a moment . . . and then pass by. But some yearning and desperate ones will be drawn to you, curious about the water that quenches your thirst.

This morning, sink your roots deeply into His Word. Drink from that well of living water. Let it cleanse your heart and yield the tender fruit of the Spirit. There are thirsty souls in your wilderness, and the Lord will lead them to you so you can guide them to His living water. As you do, your desert will become less bleak and more beautiful—and both you and they will be grateful to the One Who chose to plant you in that dry place.

92
Humble Cemetery

I was driving down a mountain valley when I spotted a little wooden sign standing in the grass: HUMBLE CEMETERY. I drove on but my mind kept wandering back.

What is a humble cemetery? Is it a modest place set way back in a hollow, rarely mowed and seldom visited? Or maybe a humble cemetery is one that makes people prove their meekness before they're allowed to buy a plot. How would they go about doing that? Would a genuinely humble person be willing to offer a tribute to his own humility? In a humble cemetery, do the meekest people get the grandest headstones? Wouldn't that be sort of contradictory?

I made a quick u-turn to follow the sign and my curiosity down a narrow lane that led through a cornfield and wound along the base of a hill along a white wooden fence. Suddenly, there it was — the Humble Cemetery — not plain at all, but a lovely place, lush with the green of a mountain summer, glowing in the late afternoon sun. And suddenly I knew what I was looking for.

I searched under tall oaks until I found it — the Humble family plot. Addie, Claude, and Clinton Humble. Fred, Hollis, Loy, and Margaret Humble. Milla, Oley, Robert, and

Ruby Humble. I read their epitaphs and wondered: were they humble in more than just name?

And I began to wish for a humble cemetery of my own. Not that I'm ready to lay my whole self to rest. I love being alive! But I would very much like a place to, once and for all, lay to rest my pride.

In a shady corner of my cemetery I'd bury my smugness, self-righteousness, and vanity. Nearby I'd dig a deep hole for my sensitivities, my love of praise and dislike of correction, and the self-focus that triggers shyness, resentment, and envy. Finally I'd bury every thought that begins with "I deserve."

Come with me. Bring along your own vanities and we'll dig holes together. When we get back home, we'll find that the ministry has become pure delight, for all the irritating ego-prickers that come from working with people will have lost their sting. We'll become famous for our humility!

If only it were that easy. The problem is that no matter how often pride is buried, it resurrects itself to reappear in the most unexpected ways and unfortunate moments. It's the original sin, so it's had a lot of practice. We'd have to return to rebury our conceit so often that we wouldn't have time to do anything else.

So if you ever spot me driving through that cornfield down the valley, you'll know where I'm going and why. Call me back. Remind me that humility can't be reached on one quick trip. It's located at the end of a long journey of dying daily for the sake of the One Who "made Himself of no reputation" (Philippians 2:7). As we travel down that road, we're gradually emptied of self and filled with Him. That's the way it works—and that's the way to the Humble Cemetery.

93
Snow Day

By birth and inclination, I'm a Southerner. And there's one thing I know about us: we know how to enjoy our snow. We may not get much of it, but we know how to make the most of it. Northerners, I've discovered, are different.

During the dozen years we pastored in the North, I learned that up there, snow simply meant that life became more inconvenient. A trip to the grocery store required stuffing wiggly children into snowsuits, boots, hats, and mittens and maneuvering balky shopping carts through parking lot ice moguls. On the drive home, the ice cream in the trunk wouldn't melt, but the lettuce would freeze. A string of heavy snowstorms didn't cause a series of cancelled church services. We went anyway, with determined smiles on our faces, and added extra cash to the offering for the drained snow removal budget.

Those tough Northerners kept plowing through the winter, going about business as usual until the white tundra slowly turned to brown (that was spring) and finally to green (that was summer). I learned to keep up with normal life no matter how icy the wind or deep the drifts, but I have to admit that I sometimes longed for one good old Southern snow day.

Southerners start preparing as soon as the local weather person hints at the possibility of flurries. We pull out our woolies from the back of the closet, check the sky often, and include the word *snow* in every conversation. And everybody, everybody, everybody runs out to buy milk and bread before it's all gone, whether we need it or not. The milk-bread run, of course, is also the time to buy popcorn, hot cocoa, chips and dip, chocolate of any variety, and ingredients for other traditional homemade snow day eats.

Then—and this is the best part—we cancel everything. By everything I mean anything that involves driving on a white-frosted street, which is a smart idea considering the creaky condition of our snow plows and the sad state of our snow removal budgets. When we've gotten everything thoroughly cancelled, we go home.

There we bundle up in comfy pajamas and triple layers of socks. We huddle on the couch cocooned in quilts. We play Uno and Dutch Blitz. We eat our snow day rations, and if enough snow actually sticks, bowls of snow cream. Occasionally somebody might dash out to measure the snow (in centimeters) or take pictures for next year's Christmas card, but we all know that the snow isn't the point. It's the unexpected vacation that matters—the impromptu family holiday, the spontaneous retreat, the sudden escape from real life into a cozy igloo. Ahhh. It's nice.

See? We Southerners really know how to enjoy our snow. When the skies clear and the snow melts (like all Southerners, our snow has good manners and never overstays its welcome), our world starts spinning again, and it's okay. We are rested, happy, and full of tales of what our family did during The Big Snow. We have talked and laughed and reconnected. We have gone on a family vacation without packing a suitcase, and it was free!

I'm thinking that once in a while, even without a flake in the forecast, we should call a personal snow day, cancel everything, and go home to huddle up, hunker down, and just be together. I don't know a single ministry family that doesn't need regular snow days away from the fishbowl life. If we keep plowing through without them, we will lose touch, lose our harmony, lose our way. With them, we renew the love that built our home and rebuild the walls of unity that shield us from outside pressures. We all need snow days to remind us of what's important.

We'll be delighted to teach you Yankees how to have a good snow day. Y'all are welcome to come down any old time, but I'd suggest a day a few months from now when the temperature and humidity make a matching pair way up in the high 90s, and we tough Southerners are going about our business as usual.

94
Portrait of You

In Romans 12:9-21, Paul painted a lovely portrait. Though it's centuries old, something about its brush strokes has always seemed familiar. As I looked at it again this morning, I realized why— it looks a lot like you!

You're the beautiful believer he paints with words, the one who loves without self-interest, who instinctively puts others before herself. You love God, too, and since you are glued to His truth, you hate sin. But your heart yearns over sinners because you know they walk a hard road. And as for the family of God—your heart and your arms are always wide open to them.

Nobody could ever call you lazy. When there's work to be done, you are there, serving Him passionately, and joyfully serving His children. You're fervent but not frantic; you're calm when it counts. When trials come, you emerge from your prayer closet with an abundance of tranquility and hope to distribute to the rest of us. When our faith fades, you share some of yours. You talk to God for us when we hurt too much to form words. You hold us together when we're falling apart.

And you put hands and feet to your prayers. You notice our needs, and if you can meet them yourself, you do. The word "inconvenient" is not in your dictionary. You feed countless friends and strangers, serving up welcoming smiles and encouraging words along with your chicken soup and cherry pie. Hospitality isn't just your ministry obligation; it's your delight. In your home, no one is ever a nuisance.

When someone decides to make herself your enemy, still you bless her in your heart, and whether friend or foe laughs or cries, you join right in. You never hold yourself apart or climb up onto the pedestal of your ministry title. Instead, you sit where we sit. You're never conceited; a snob, you're not. In your world, no one is an outcast.

No matter how you are treated, revenge is the last thing on your mind. You'd much rather turn foes into friends and competitors into companions. You thaw frozen hearts with the warmth of your love. You rise above instead of getting even, for you trust the One Who promises to work "righteousness and judgment for all that are oppressed" (Psalm 103:6).

You counter grumpiness with good humor and crabbiness with cheer. You calm the cantankerous and soothe the surly. You brighten our world, sustain our spirit, and lighten our load. I really don't know what we would do without you.

Paul has not yet met you, my friend, but someday he will, and on that heavenly day I'm sure he'll agree with me: when he wrote Romans 12:9-21, he was painting a picture of you.

About the Author

Claudia Barba grew up in the home of parents who loved the Lord and served Him in ministry, making it look like such a joyful life that all three of their daughters married preachers. After graduating from a Christian university and completing graduate school, Claudia married Dave Barba, knowing she would never be bored.

The Barbas have planted and pastored two churches and traveled with their family in itinerant evangelism. In 2001, their children grown with children of their own, Dave and Claudia began traveling once more, assisting church planters through a ministry they call *Press On! Ministries*.

Claudia is the author of Bible study books for women, including *Refresh Your Heart* and *When Christ Was Here,* published by Journey Forth Books. Dave's book *Press On!* is an encouraging resource for men in ministry. You can follow their church planting adventure by visiting their website: www.ipresson.com.

The Barbas have seen God prove true this promise they claimed long ago: *"Faithful is He that calleth you, Who also will do it"* (1 Thessalonians 5:24). They enjoy living by faith in the faithful One and look forward to serving Him every day until He comes.